SPACE AGE DESIGN

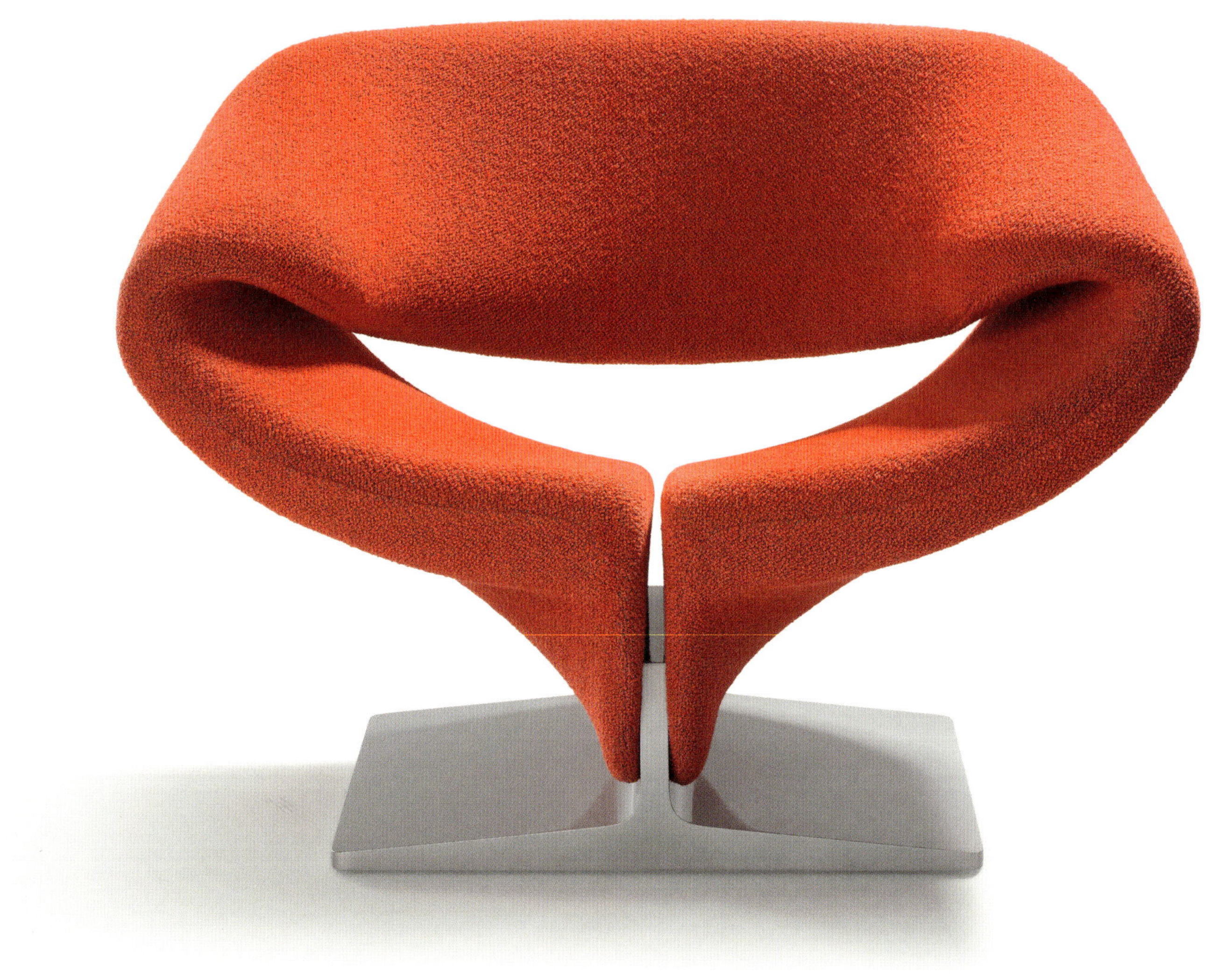

Ribbon Chair, Pierre Paulin for Artifort, 1966

Peter Martin

SPACE AGE DESIGN

Icons of the movement

teNeues

ISTI#1, Kosmic Memories, 2021. Courtesy of the artist Vincent Fournier.
Work depicts the Kyiv Institute of Information, USSR, 1971

CONTENTS

Challenger Space Shuttle launches from Cape Canaveral

INTRODUCTION

On a freezing January morning in 1986, the Space Shuttle Challenger lifted off from Cape Canaveral and began to ascend into a cobalt-blue Florida sky. Thousands had congregated in the launch zone below as this was no ordinary flight; a civilian was on board—a teacher, as part of a program to engage young people—and millions of children gathered at screens around the world in a way not seen since the days of Apollo.

Moments later, the shuttle exploded into a nebula that stretched across the sky. The crowd below watched in stunned silence, then in horror as it became clear that something catastrophic had happened.

Everyone at school at the time remembers the day the seven astronauts were vaporized live on television. Some might remember President Ronald Reagan's eulogy that night: "They had a hunger to explore the universe and discover its truths.... We'll continue our quest in space. Nothing ends here."

But something did end there. The Challenger Disaster didn't end space exploration, but it marked a final close to the mid-20th-century Space Age—an era of optimism, innovation, and intense creative energy.

Three decades earlier, humans had embarked on an epochal endeavor. From the 1950s to the 1980s, space exploration, the space race, and all of the penumbra around it exerted an extraordinary influence on culture. Throughout the mid-century era, it was a glittering thread weaving through everyone's lives. My generation was shaped by it. Our older siblings had witnessed the first moon landing, and we grew up on a diet of *Star Trek*, *Star Wars,* and *Space Invaders,* with an understanding that we'd all be holidaying on the moon by the year 2000.

Later, I became captivated by the design from the period. Mid-century design has an addictive and persistent hold on contemporary audiences anyway; but there is an additional magic about the furniture, products, fashion, and architecture that grew out of the Space Age. To many living now, the future looks unsettling. In the late 1950s, the future was a place of dreams. Cars grew rocket-like tailfins, airports were modeled on spaceships. Futurism influenced furniture. It was an age of optimism—even utopianism—and it reverberated throughout Western culture, from fashion and music to design and art.

Just as society was glimpsing the future through the prism of the Space Age and reconsidering how we might live and structure our lives, new materials were upending the possibilities of what could be created. Advanced forms of plastic, fiberglass, and plywood, developed through the war years, began to find their way into the workshops of a new generation of designers. Revolutionary products seduced consumers with notions of how one might live in this new era of space travel.

This was the backdrop to what can now be called Space Age Design—the work of a generation of designers, architects, and creatives at a time when a cultural revolution was underway and the space race was both its catalyst and its muse. It's a movement with fuzzy borders, overlapping palimpsests of many other schools from Modernism to Atomic Age. But a movement it is, borne out of a distinct moment in our cultural history. While designers such as Eero Saarinen, Joe Colombo, Pierre Paulin, and Verner Panton transcend labels, their body of work provides a lens into a now-departed world of mid-century ebullience. And in turn, the unique political, economic, cultural, and scientific circumstances of the Space Age provide a lens through which we can better understand and appreciate the seminal works of some of the most innovative designers of the modern era.

Los Angeles International Airport (LAX) Theme Building circa 1961

SPUTNIK TO GAGARIN 1957–1961

PART I

There was only one place to be in Washington D.C. on the warm evening of 4 October 1957. Marking the conclusion of a successful conference for International Geophysical Year, a cocktail party was getting underway in the elegant halls of the National Academy of Sciences. In a room hazy with cigarette and cigar smoke, Soviet physicists in coarse wool suits brushed shoulders with German geologists and American State Department officials.

But below the academic gossip and clinking of martini glasses lay a thick undercurrent of conjecture, even dread.

Suddenly, the atmosphere tightened. Speculation spread out across the room like electricity. Walter Sullivan, the *New York Times* science reporter, entered and scanned the room until his eyes settled on American physicist Lloyd Berkner, president of the International Council of Scientific Unions (and the man former NASA Chief Historian Roger D. Launius describes as having "his fingerprints all over every big U.S. science activity between World War Two and the mid-1960s"). The reporter weaved through the crowd with urgency, gripped Berkner's shoulder, and whispered two words in his ear to describe the event that was about to change the world: "It's up."

High above them, a shiny metal object was shooting across North America at 10 times the speed of a bullet. It sliced across the Pacific to Asia, the Soviet Union, and on into orbit, emitting a persistent signal that would soon be heard by radio receivers around the world.

Minutes earlier, the Soviet news agency TASS had issued a press release: the USSR had successfully launched the world's first orbiting artificial satellite—Sputnik.

As word rippled across the planet, millions instinctively looked upwards. News stations everywhere broadcast the radio signal that would become one of the most recognized sounds of a generation. Billions would remember exactly where they were when they first heard the news. Almost everyone alive at the time sensed that humanity had entered a new phase of existence.

Sputnik's effects were immediate and profound. In the United States, the thrill of a new age of space exploration was accompanied by alarm that the Soviets had got there first. Thomas Hamilton, who a decade later would work on the Apollo program, remembers the atmosphere the morning after: "People on the subway line in New York City were staring in horror at their newspapers. Nothing like it since Pearl Harbor."

Across the West, the idea that the Soviet Union could soon have the ability to launch spy satellites over Nevada, or drop atomic bombs from space onto London or Los Angeles, was perceived as an existential threat. "What is at stake is nothing less than our survival," proclaimed Democratic senator Mike Mansfield. In the battle of ideas between democracy and communism, the thought that Khrushchev's threat to the United States a year earlier that "we will bury you" might actually be happening fomented a deep panic that became known as the Sputnik Crisis. And the Sputnik Crisis ignited the Space Race.

THE WORLD IN 1957

What was it like to be alive on that October night of Sputnik in 1957?

As the Soviet satellite began its ascent, Alfred Hitchcock was filming *Vertigo* with James Stewart and Kim Novak in San Francisco. Buddy Holly's *That'll be the Day* was at the top of the U.S. Billboard charts. American soldiers had gradually returned home from Europe after the Second World War to a strident economy; the baby boom was underway and the American Dream had never looked so achievable. A shattered European continent was recovering and rebuilding; and in the UK, war rationing had finally ended. The Cold War had created a new sense of unity and purpose in the West. Behind the Iron Curtain, Khrushchev offered the prospect of a post-Stalin dialing down of tension. Ghana had become the first sub-Saharan country to gain independence six months earlier; and across Africa and Asia, decolonization was beginning its journey towards its 1960 peak.

As for space, it's hard to imagine now, with our Mars rovers, space stations, thousands of satellites, and probes throughout the solar system, how remote that future seemed in 1957. No one had seen the world from space. The iconic blue marble we are now so familiar with had never been photographed. Many still believed Mars was covered with vegetation—and possibly harboring intelligent life. Images of planets were fuzzy, shot through earthbound telescopes, and while the rings of Saturn or the bands of Jupiter could be picked out, there was no detail, and no hint of what lay beneath the clouds.

INTERIORS

To leaf through a copy of *Architectural Digest* in 1957 was to see a world at the height of Mid-century Modern. Homes in Bel Air, Coconut Grove, and Palm Springs were open-plan playgrounds of exposed brickwork, free-standing fireplaces, geometric lines, and floor-to-ceiling windows. Kitchens were fitted, the stoves electric. Notes of golden-era Hollywood Regency were still visible—clamshell chairs and sunburst clocks. It wasn't a monoculture—the Vanderbilt penthouse in New York in 1957 featured more pre-war decorativeness than would be fashionable on the West Coast. But the trend was clear: it was clean, pared-back, Modernist, airy. That's not to say austere—the post-war prosperity was filtering through in vibrant mint greens, pinks, teal, and chartreuse.

One of the most famous residences to be completed in 1957 was the Miller House in Indiana, by architect and designer Eero Saarinen (whose sculptural Tulip Chair is one of the foremost icons of Space-Age design). The property epitomizes many classic aspects of Modernist interior architecture—expansive glass and concrete walls, a cylindrical fireplace, an open layout, and a sunken conversation pit: a large area on a lower level in the living room lined by a modular sofa. The Miller House—and the properties in 1957's *Architectural Digest*—did not, of course, reflect how most people in Europe and America lived, but they certainly showed the direction of travel for those who could afford it.

"But the trend was clear: it was clean, pared-back, Modernist, airy."

A DESIGN REVOLUTION

In the years leading up to 1957, a revolution in furniture and product design had been unfolding—a three-headed revolution that enabled the explosion of Space-Age influence of the late 1950s and beyond.

The first was a revolution in materials. Fiberglass, plywood, and plastic had undergone major innovations during the war and increased availability in the years following it; and these materials were the fuel that would power a new generation of designers.

Plastic would have the profoundest effect. Plastic itself was not new—Bakelite had been invented in 1907 and was commonplace by the 1920s. But during the war, new plastics such as ABS and polyethylene emerged—thermal plastics that were less brittle, more malleable, and far easier to produce. With the war effort on both sides consuming natural resources, this created a major opportunity for petrochemical companies to step in and create ersatz wood and metal out of their new products.

Plywood also took on greater importance. New, stronger forms were used in air assault gliders and fighter aircraft. Two young designers, Charles and Ray Eames, both spent time during the war developing plywood for military applications such as leg and arm splints for injured soldiers. After the war, the Eames applied these new processes to furniture production.

Furniture makers had been molding plywood with steam since Michel Thonet pioneered the Bentwood Chair in Vienna in the 1850s. But the Eames elevated it to the level of sculpture. "I look at the Eames as a 2D versus 3D story," says Johanna Agerman Ross, chief curator of the London Design Museum. "Before the Eames, plywood was usually shaped in two planes. The Eames began experimenting with forming sculptural shapes in three dimensions. They gave a hint of what was to come." There followed a radical liberation of what could be imagined as furniture; and what the Eames had begun with plywood accelerated with fiberglass and plastic. "In the 1950s, plastic represented possibilities, freedom, and joy," says Cristina Bargna, head of the *Plastic Design Collection* at Design Museum Brussels. "The freedom of shape; the possibility to create new furniture, to furnish new houses—a material that spoke to a new generation with the desire to live differently. Plastic was no longer a material that imitated what had come before. It started to embody the future; it created a completely new vision of reality."

"Before the Eames, plywood was usually shaped in two planes. The Eames began experimenting with forming sculptural shapes in three dimensions. They gave a hint of what was to come."

A MOMENT OF MASS

The second pillar of the design revolution was the post-war explosion in mass production.

The war economy in the United States and Europe had acted as a massive adrenaline shot for industry, and this now pivoted towards a burgeoning consumer culture. The U.S. finished the war with a well-primed manufacturing base and an economic boom. In Europe, the Marshall Plan injected $13.6 billion ($150 billion adjusted for today) into the continent's shattered economies. By the time of Sputnik, West Germany was undergoing an economic miracle, and France, Britain, and Italy had weathered the worst of the post-war slump. Western consumers were ready for mass production, and product and furniture design were undergoing a profound shift of emphasis from creating just a few unique objects to creating at scale for the masses. And while this arrangement was ideal for manufacturers pivoting from the war economies, it was also a genuine moment of symbiosis between them and the designers who embraced the opportunity to change the way millions could live.

"This idea of serving a wider audience was something that was on all of these designers' minds," says Agerman Ross. "The collaboration between them and the manufacturers suited both, and there was no feeling of anyone being taken advantage of as everyone was on a similar trajectory."

This relationship between designer and manufacturer was the third driver of the design revolution. The Eames did not just lay the groundwork for the designers of the space-race era in terms of pioneering and harnessing new materials. They also redefined what it meant to be a designer in a way that opened the door for the post-Sputnik designers that were to follow. The story of Space-Age design is in many ways a story of partnership between designers and manufacturers. Joe Colombo with Kartell; Eero Saarinen with Knoll; Verner Panton with Vitra; Peter Ghyczy with Elastogran. In the Eameses case, their partnership with Herman Miller and the Evans Products Company had created the blueprint.

FROM SPUTNIK TO GAGARIN

Roger D. Launius describes the effect the launch of Sputnik 1 had on American public opinion as "a shock, introducing the average citizen to the Space Age in a crisis setting." The *New York Times* alone ran 279 articles about the satellite in October 1957.

Launius goes on to say: "Almost immediately, two phrases entered the American lexicon to define time: 'pre-Sputnik' and 'post-Sputnik.' The other phrase that soon replaced earlier definitions of time was 'Space Age.' With the launch of Sputnik 1, the Space Age had been born and the world would be different ever after."

But a further shock awaited. On 3 November 1957, less than a month after Sputnik 1 and before President Eisenhower could formulate any coherent response, the Soviet Union marked the 40th anniversary of the Russian Revolution by blasting Laika, a female dog, into orbit inside Sputnik 2.

Khrushchev had ordered his engineers to deliver a "space spectacular" that would stun the world. And it was a major win for Soviet prestige, cementing the global impression that the communists were technologically advanced and winning the space race.

Laika's space flight intensely increased the pressure on Eisenhower. The U.S. president had maintained that, as part of International Geophysical Year, both sides in the Cold War had openly stated their intention to put satellites into orbit; and while the Russians had pipped them to it, it was all part of the plan and nothing to be alarmed at. But that view was not shared by many in his own administration; and the Democrats, under Senate majority leader Lyndon B. Johnson, shrewdly sensed an opportunity to portray Eisenhower as weak and unprepared. Encouraged by the Democrats, the feeling was taking hold that the President had been caught asleep at the wheel. And it was about to get worse.

"Almost immediately, two phrases entered the American lexicon to define time: 'pre-Sputnik' and 'post-Sputnik.' The other phrase that soon replaced earlier definitions of time was 'Space Age.' With the launch of Sputnik 1, the Space Age had been born and the world would be different ever after."

THE VANGUARD DISASTER

On 6 December 1957, the world's media arrived in Cape Canaveral to witness the launch of Vanguard TV-3—America's answer to Sputnik. It was a major moment that heralded America's entry into the space race and thousands turned up to watch.

At 16:45, the booster ignited and the rocket began to rise. But seconds later, it froze in mid-air, just above the launchpad, before sagging strangely and then collapsing as if its skeleton had been vaporized. As onlookers struggled to grasp what they were seeing, the rocket then vanished in a colossal orange fire cloud that engulfed the entire launch site.

It was a very public humiliation. Next to the dazzling success of Sputnik, the media were quick to dub Vanguard "Flopnik" and "Kaputnik". It was a bitter blow to American prestige; days later, the Soviets sardonically asked the United Nations to consider if the U.S. might qualify for aid for "undeveloped countries".

Vanguard's failure and the Soviet launch of Laika galvanized the U.S. administration, who were under intense pressure from the Democrats and keenly aware of the geopolitical danger of ceding prestige to their global rival. Eisenhower responded with a rapid acceleration of the space program, tapping Wernher von Braun, now the chief architect of the U.S. Army's space rocket program, which had been developing in parallel to the Navy's Vanguard program. And on 31 January 1958, von Braun's Juno rocket launched America's first satellite, Explorer 1, into orbit. The United States had demonstrated to the world that it was a serious contender. The space race was on.

ATOMIUM

In the spring of 1958, as the United States planned out its next steps in the space race, one of Europe's strangest structures was receiving its final polish. The Atomium in Brussels is a Modernist landmark, modeled on nine iron atoms magnified 165 billion times. Still one of the tallest buildings in Belgium, it was constructed as the centerpiece of Expo 58—the 1958 Brussels World's Fair. It's one of the boldest monuments to have been created in the 20th century, and it's a masterpiece of Space-Age design in its futurism and idealistic optimism about the potential of science to advance humankind.

Aesthetically, it never disappoints. Against a blue sky, the sun glints off the highest stainless steel spheres with an uncanny sharpness; when overcast, the Atomium rises out of the mist like an alien invasion. It's a perfectly preserved slice of a vanished Cold War world.

Expo 58 was itself a manifestation of global rivalry at the cusp of the space race. Visitors to the imposing Soviet pavilion at the foot of the Atomium would ascend the marble steps to find a gleaming prototype of Sputnik suspended at the center of the cavernous hall, the gaze of a monolithic statue of Lenin upon it. The message to the world was clear: the USSR was a technological superpower. In its own pavilion, the United States—at this point perceived as an also-ran in the space race—chose to instead project the allure of its unmatched consumer culture: a fashion show; color television; Walt Disney.

But it was the Soviet pavilion that was awarded the expo's Grand Prix. The Soviets had already understood the enormous propaganda value of achievement in space.

"The Atomium in Brussels is a Modernist landmark, modeled on nine iron atoms magnified 165 billion times."

ARNE JACOBSEN

A few hundred miles across Europe, another of the era's iconic shapes was being launched. By 1958, Arne Jacobsen was already one of Denmark's most celebrated architects; he had achieved acclaim for his House of the Future in 1929 and Aarhus City Hall in 1942. While Jacobsen never described himself as a designer, he had begun collaborating with furniture manufacturer Republic of Fritz Hansen in 1934 and had created several bestselling classics still in production today, including 1952's Ant Chair, a stackable three-legged chair sculpted from a single piece of plywood.

However, it's the 1958 Egg Chair that was destined to be Jacobsen's most recognizable work, one that is now globally acknowledged as an icon of furniture design. Even its silhouette is enough to evoke the élan of an entire era, and it's become an emblem of Space-Age design.

Sculpted from a hard foam material which was then padded and upholstered, Jacobsen created the Egg for the architect's SAS Royal Hotel. Described as "the world's first Design Hotel" (as well as Copenhagen's first skyscraper), it was equally notable at the time for the way Jacoben's Egg, Swan, and Drop chairs were integrated throughout the lobby and rooms as part of the architect's adherence to "total design". While all traces of Jacobsen's original interior scheme have now been ripped out, Room 606 at what is now called the Radisson Collection Royal Hotel has been restored by Norm Architects to Jacobsen's original plans, complete with a powder-blue version of the Egg Chair that exerted such influence on the future of furniture design.

SPACE-AGE CARS

Throughout this period, a fantasy version of space travel exerted an extraordinary influence on 1950s culture. For a decade, cars had been sprouting rocket-like fins and space-ship styling. The 1952 Alfa Romeo Disco Volante took its shape and name from a flying saucer. The rocket-shaped Ghia Gilda, debuting at the 1955 Turin Salone dell'Automobile, created such a buzz that it inspired Virgil Exner, Chrysler's Vice President of Design, to draw up the car giant's 1957 "Forward Look" style guidelines. As a result, Chrysler's Dodge, Plymouth, De Soto, and Imperial divisions were all given futuristic tailfins; so receptive was the U.S. market to this jet-age and Space-Age styling that Chrysler's market share grew almost 20 percent.

In response, their rival General Motors gave us the car that has become visual shorthand for the Dreamboat era—the 1959 Cadillac Eldorado Biarritz, with its extravagant rocket fins and tail lights. Jason Barlow, in his book *The Atlas of Car Design*, describes it as "an arrogant, overblown ode to excess"—though he concedes that "it's impossible not to marvel at it." Whatever one thinks of it, the Biarritz gives us a glimpse into that late-1950s moment in America when space and futurism went mainstream.

OSCAR NIEMEYER'S BRASILIA

If car models are emissaries of past moments, the stakes are that much higher in public buildings designed to last generations. Yet the architecture of the period throws up extraordinary examples of Space-Age influence, perhaps none more so than Oscar Niemeyer's Modernist masterpiece, Brasília—an entire Space-Age capital city, created from scratch in the late 1950s deep in the highlands of Brazil. When the Russian cosmonaut Yuri Gagarin visited Brasília, he described it as "like arriving on another planet."

Vincent Fournier is the author of *Brasília—A Time Capsule* and a visual artist whose images of Brasília hang in the New York MET's permanent collection. Fournier says: "Oscar Niemeyer's city embodies the vision of the future inherited from the 1950s and 60s. The pilot plan, conceived in 1957 by the urban planner Lucio Costa, coincides with the beginning of the Space Age and the first artificial satellite, Sputnik. It was therefore the golden age of the Space Age, and the city of Brasília—with its air of a flying saucer landed in the middle of nowhere—expresses the nostalgia and the dream of a future that remains frozen in time."

"Oscar Niemeyer's city embodies the vision of the future inherited from the 1950s and 60s."

PROJECT MERCURY AND THE BIRTH OF NASA

Following the flight of the Soviet dog Laika, it was clear to both the Soviets and the Americans that the next clear goal in the space race was human spaceflight. For the Soviets, this meant the Vostok program, led by chief designer Sergei Korolev. For the Americans, Project Mercury was created to address the objective of putting a human into orbit and returning them safely.

Mercury had originally been planned as a military program, and it was conceived inside the Department of Defence before NASA existed. When NASA was being established in the summer of 1958, the military fought hard to keep hold of it, and Mercury began operations—under the military—on 1 October.

But Eisenhower had other plans. "Eisenhower, to his credit, recognized that Mercury would be more useful as an international political tool if it was public, and was operated by a non-threatening entity," says Roger D. Launius. "NASA was always viewed in that category—and it was set up to be in that category. So, moving Mercury to NASA meant that they could then very publicly talk about it, and play it for all it was worth in the public's perceptions. And NASA did it beautifully."

There's no better example of this than the unveiling of the "Mercury 7", as the seven astronauts selected for the program became known, at a press conference in Washington D.C. on 9 April 1959. It's one of the major milestones of the space race, and it's mesmerizing to watch this early piece of staged PR as it marks a shift not just in the space race itself, but in global mainstream culture. The seven quintessential fighter jocks had had no media training or experience, but they found themselves catapulted into a completely unexpected vortex of celebrity mayhem. In the film, they sit there, awkward in their suits and bowties, nervously smoking cigarettes as they face the media pack. Walter T. Bonney, NASA's first director of the office of public information, steps up to the microphone and pulls on his own cigarette as he introduces the astronauts. He says "astronaut" self-consciously, as if they're still testing out the word.

The press conference ignited a frenzy of interest. In contrast to coverage of rocket launches and orbital data, it was the human story that truly lit the world's imagination. *Life Magazine*, in its extensive coverage, introduced the Mercury 7 in portentous language:

"Some fine early morning before another summer has come, one man chosen from the calmly intent seven ... will embark on the greatest adventure man has ever dared to take.... If he survives, he will become the heroic symbol of a historic triumph; he will be the first American, perhaps the first man, to be rocketed into the dark stillness of space. If he does not survive, one of his six remaining comrades will go next."

From this point on, while the USSR's Vostok was inching forward in secrecy, the American space program had faces: John Glenn, Wally Schirra, Alan Shepard, and the rest of their crewmates. “They became public figures in ways that not even NASA had envisioned,” says Launius. “But when each of them got applauded every time they showed up in a room, it became clear to NASA that they had a powerful tool for public opinion.”

As the 1960s began, both superpowers were racking up space “firsts” and there was a sense that perhaps the race was evening out. America’s Discoverer 13 was the first satellite to be recovered intact from orbit; Discoverer 14 marked the first spy photography from space. The Soviets returned two dogs alive from orbit, and the United States returned Ham—a chimpanzee—from space.

Then came 1961, which would emerge as a pivotal year in the space race. In January, John F. Kennedy was inaugurated as President of the United States. In the same month, Alan Shepard was chosen to crew America’s first mission into space. Following rigorous training, a date was set for 6 March 1961. But fatefully, the flight that would have taken Alan Shepard out of Earth’s atmosphere and into history was delayed.

Instead, on 12 April 1961, Soviet cosmonaut Yuri Gagarin became the first human in space.

Soviet cosmonaut Yuri Gagarin, the first human in space, aboard Vostok 1, 1961

Space research: (above) Researcher at the NASA Lewis Research Center with a model of a nuclear-propelled rocket, 1961. (right) Supersonic propulsion wind tunnel at the National Advisory Committee for Aeronautics (NACA) Lewis Flight Propulsion Laboratory, mid-1950s

Sputnik, the world's first artificial satellite, launched by the Soviet Union on 4 October 1957
(replica from the National Air and Space Museum, Washington D.C.)

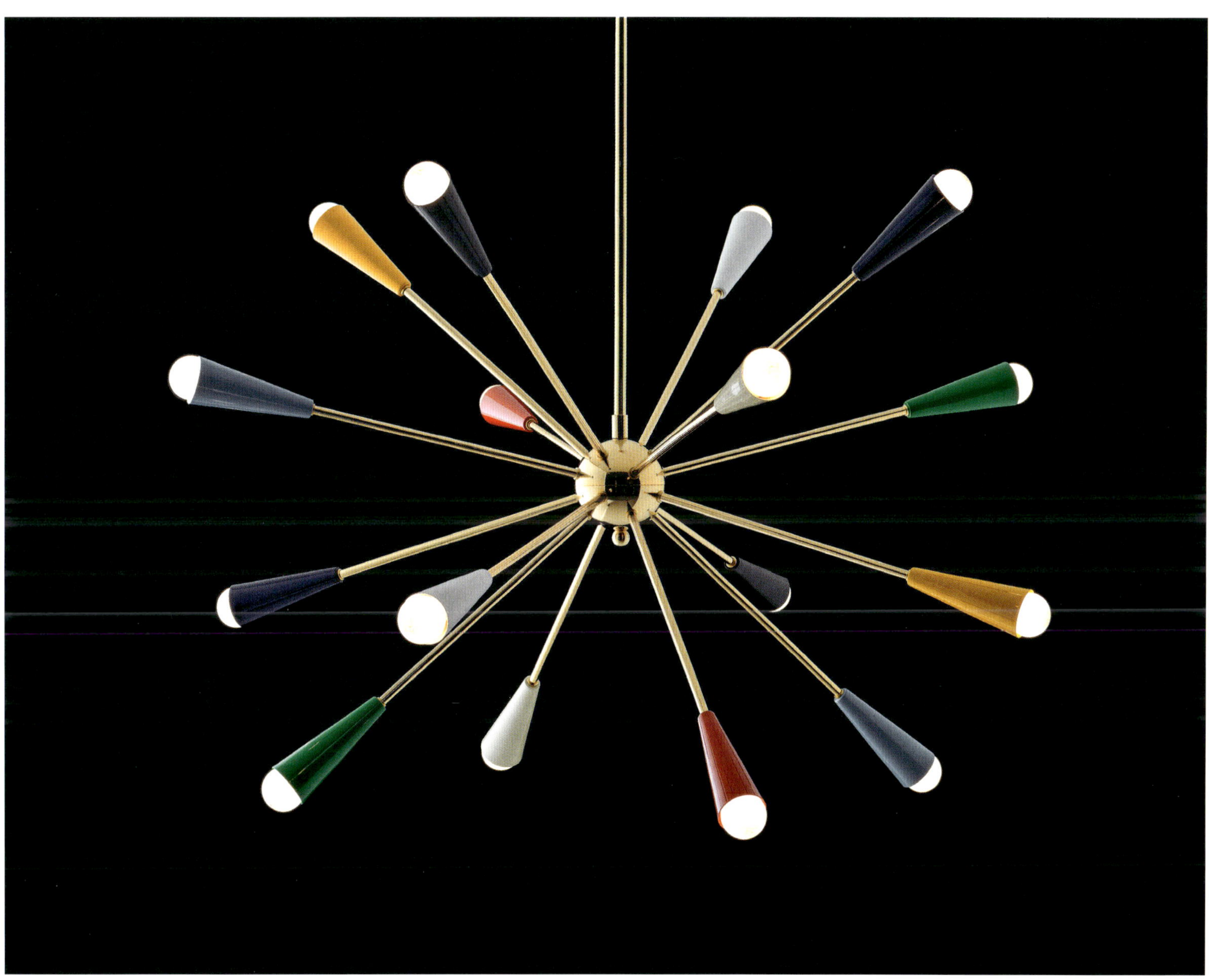

Sputnik Sospensione Chandelier by Stilnovo, Italy, designed in 1957

Miss Baker, payload of Jupiter (AM-18), on a model of the Jupiter rocket. Miss Baker was a squirrel monkey who, together with a rhesus macaque, became one of the first two animals launched into space and safely returned home by the United States Space Program in May 1959

Dr. Wernher von Braun, director of the Marshall Space Flight Center (MSFC), pictured at his desk in 1960. The German-American von Braun was one of the world's leading rocket pioneers, aerospace engineers, and space architects during WWII and throughout the space-race era

Launch of Little Joe booster (LJ1B) from Wallops Island, Virginia, on a Project Mercury test mission, January 1960

Monument to the Conquerors of Space, Moscow, conceived 1958; completed 1964

Space-Age architecture: An exuberant example of Space-Age airport design is the Theme Building at Los Angeles International Airport (right and page 8/9). Built between 1957 and 1961, it's a building of almost outrageous élan, a paean to the optimism and exploratory sensibility of the early Space-Age era. Another prime example of space-inspired architecture in Los Angeles is John Lautner's 1960 Chemosphere House (above). Like a UFO perched over a cliff, it was described by a contemporaneous *Encyclopædia Britannica* as "the most modern home built in the world."

(top) Chemosphere House, Los Angeles by architect John Lautner, completed in 1960

(top) Los Angeles International Airport (LAX) Theme Building during construction, circa 1960.
(bottom) The completed Theme Building in 1965

Eero Saarinen's General Motors Technical Center, Michigan, photographed in 1956.
The press at the time described the complex as 'an industrial Versailles'.

Luna Verticale floor lamp, designed by Gio Ponti in 1957

Eero Saarinen's TWA Flight Center, New York, constructed 1956–62

(top and above) Eero Saarinen's TWA Flight Center in New York, constructed 1956–62

Eero Saarinen's Space-Age TWA Flight Center in New York began construction in 1956, eventually opening in 1962. Described by the architect and author Donald Albrecht as "a modern-day Statue of Liberty that welcomed people to America's financial and cultural capital," it was a palace of soaring, Space-Age design emblematic of the confidence that characterized America at that moment. The TWA Flight Center operated as terminal until 2001; it has now been fully restored and repurposed as the TWA Hotel, with the original styling and Space-Age furniture, including Eero Saarinen's Tulip-series tables and chairs.

Eero Saarinen's TWA Flight Center exterior circa 1962

National Congress of Brazil #2, Brasília, 2019. Courtesy of the artist Vincent Fournier. Work depicts Brasília, designed by Oscar Niemeyer 1957–60

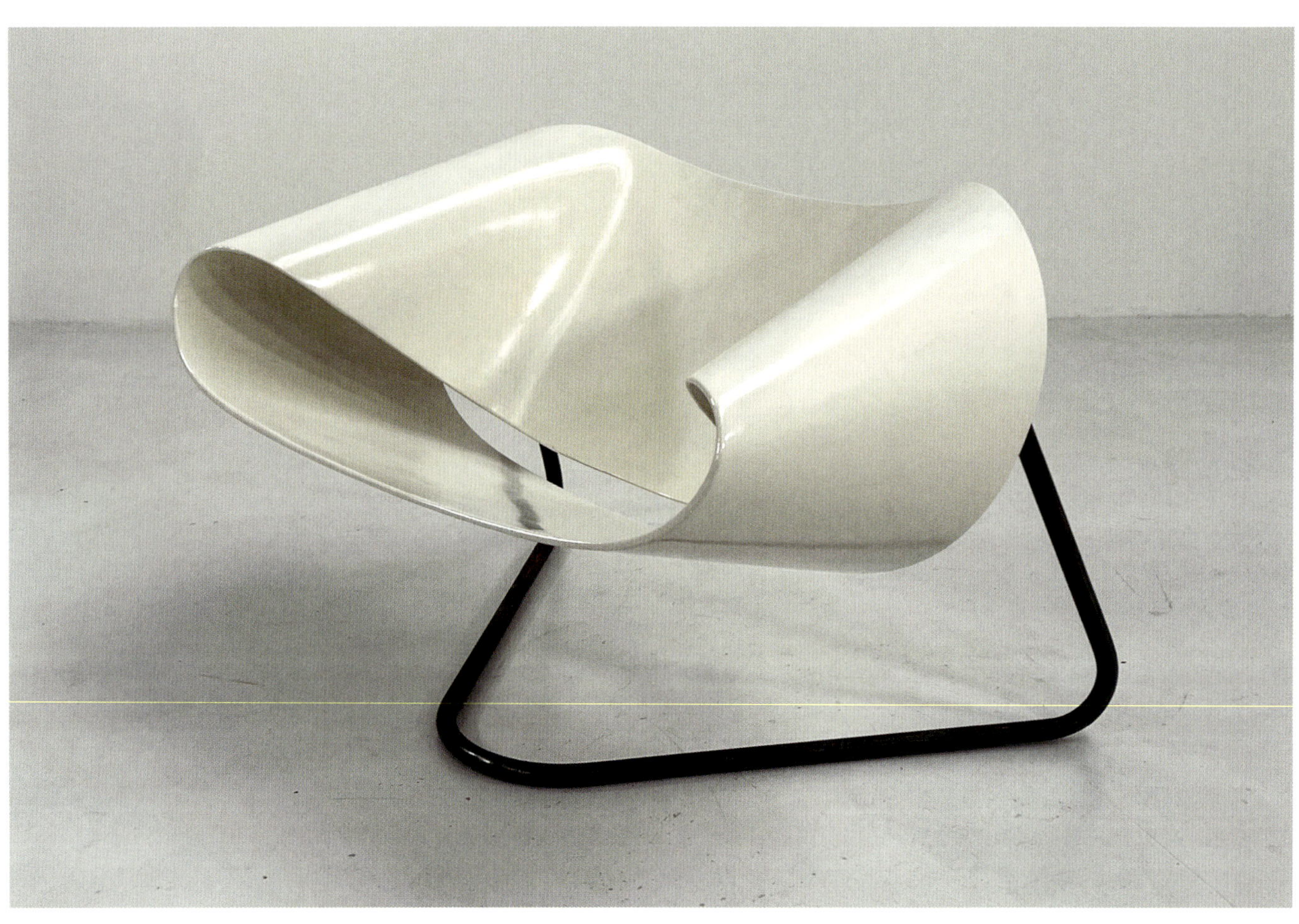

Model CL9 Ribbon Chair in molded fiberglass on chrome tubular base by Cesare Leonardi and Franca Stagi for Bernini, 1961
(courtesy Kooloo Modern)

Palácio da Alvorada #1, Brasília, 2019. Courtesy of the artist Vincent Fournier.
The National Museum #3, Brasília, 2019. Courtesy of the artist Vincent Fournier.
Works depict Brasília, designed by Oscar Niemeyer 1957–60

Chamber of Deputies [annex IX] #2 Brasília 2012. Courtesy of the artist Vincent Fournier.
Work depicts Brasília, designed by Oscar Niemeyer 1957-60

A precursor to the shapeshifting era of Space-Age design: the Marshmallow Sofa, designed by George Nelson for Knoll, 1956

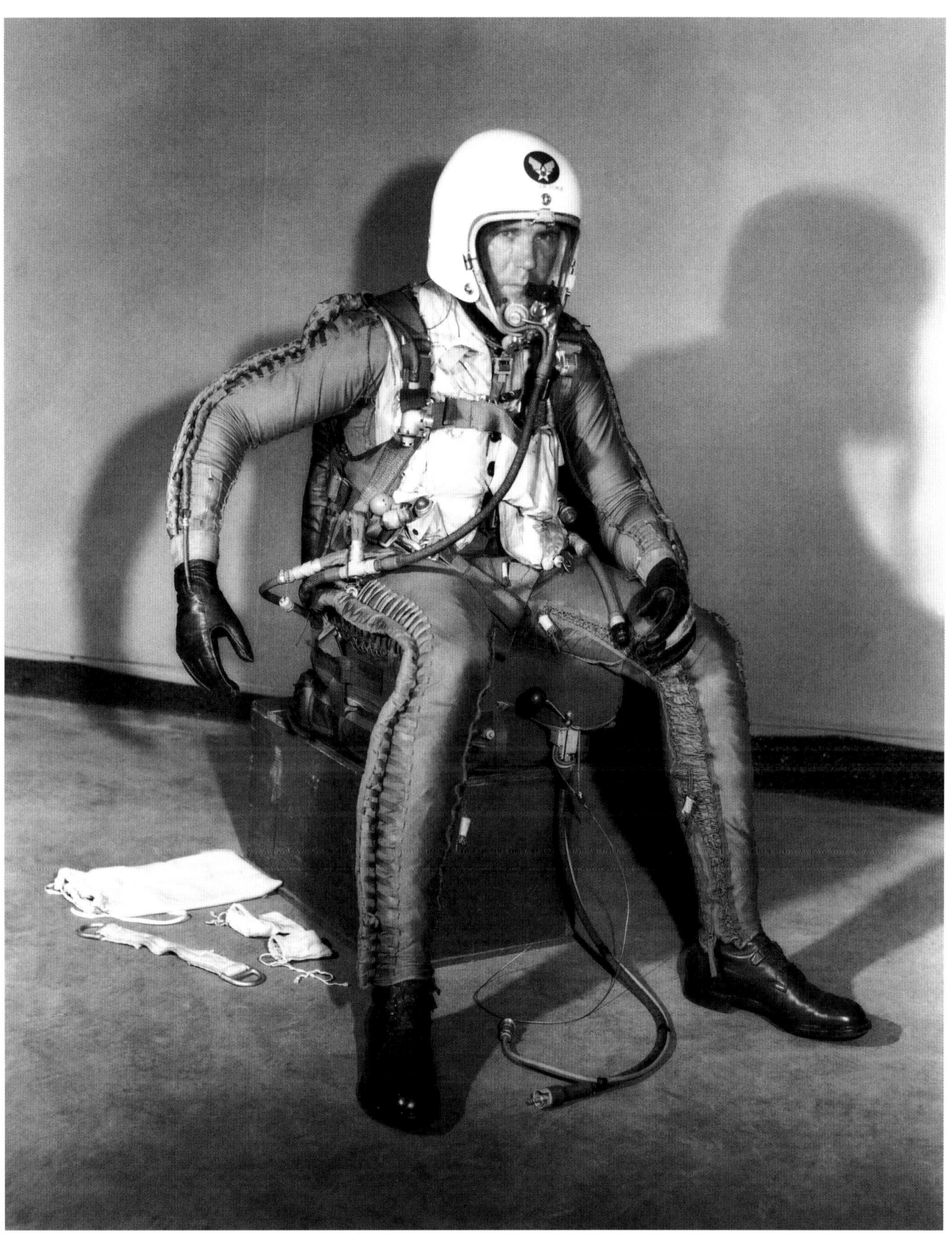

Experimental test pilot Robert Champine in an X-Series pressure suit, 1958 (Morentz)

Danish architect Arne Jacobsen's 1958 Egg Chair is one of the most emblematic chairs of the Space-Age era. Sculpted from a hard foam material which was then padded and upholstered, Jacobsen designed it for his SAS Royal Hotel, Copenhagen's first skyscraper, which also opened in 1958. The hotel integrated Jacobsen's Egg, Swan, and Drop chairs throughout the lobby and bedrooms as part of the architect's adherence to "total design".

Egg, Swan, and Drop chairs in Arne Jacobsen's SAS Hotel, Copenhagen, designed in 1958

Arne Jacobsen for Fritz Hansen, early Egg model 3316 lounge chair in leather and steel, Denmark, designed in 1958 (Morentz)

Atomium, Belgium, constructed for the 1958 Brussels World's Fair

Brussels World's Fair (Expo 58) with the Atomium in the background, 1958

Original promotional image of the Orange Slice Chair, designed by Pierre Paulin for Artifort in 1960

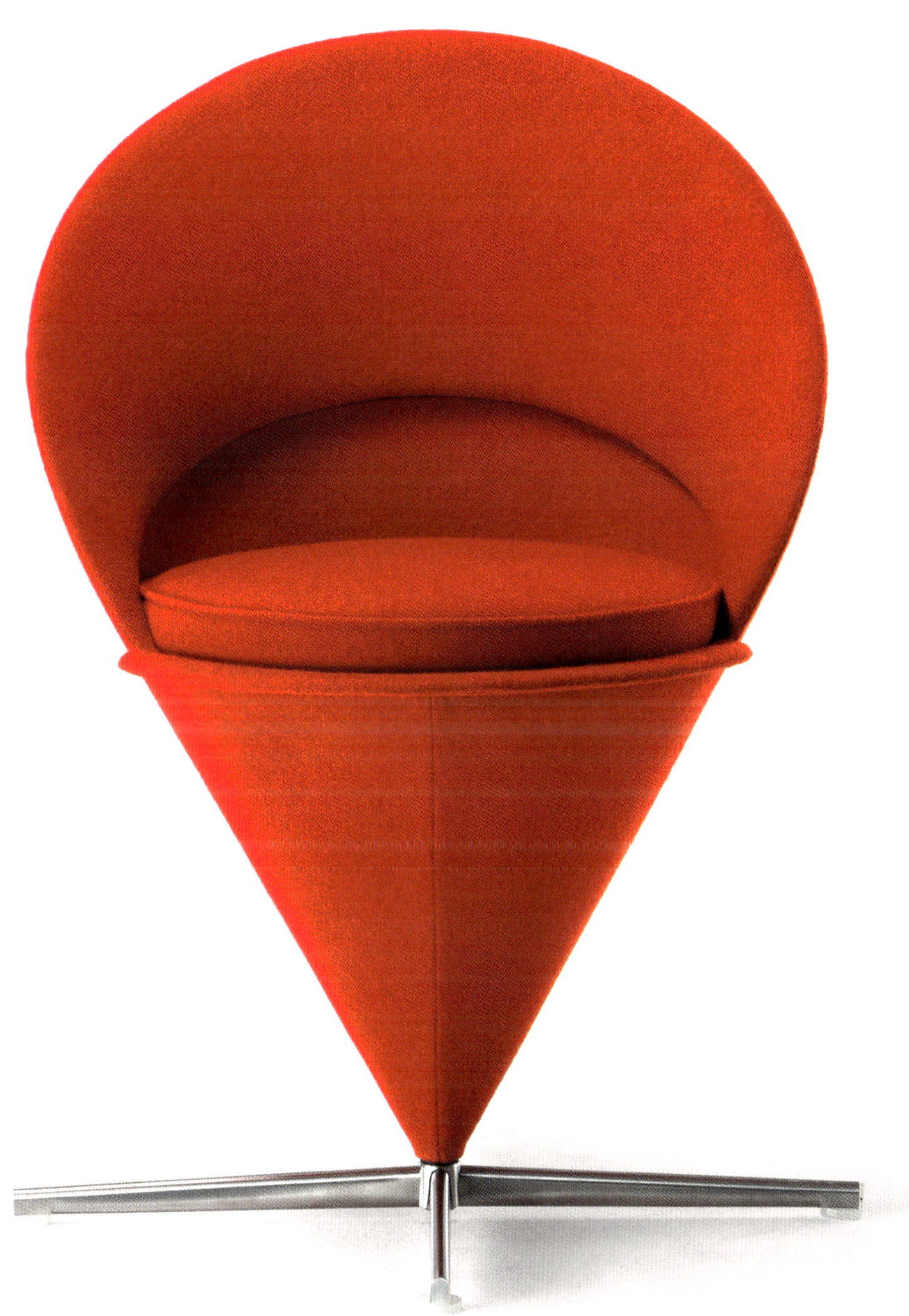

Cone Chair, designed by Verner Panton in 1958 © Vitra

Verner Panton's 1958 Cone Chair series, including the Cone (previous page), the Heart Cone (above, with Verner Panton seated), and the K2 Wire Cone (right), are among the Danish architect and designer's most iconic works. "It was the optical lightness—the apparent floating of the Cone chair balancing on a single point—that intrigued him," says his daughter, Carin Panton von Halem.

The chair was first unveiled in 1958 at the Kom-igen Inn, which Panton had redesigned in radical fashion; and the chair drew great international attention—when the Cone series was first displayed in a New York shop window, the futuristic designs reputedly caused a commotion in the streets. The Cone Chair is still produced today by Vitra.

(above left) Design by Verner Panton, www.verner-panton.com © Verner Panton Design AG.
(above right) Courtesy Vitra

K2 Wire Cone Chair (1959–60) for Plus-linje, with Moon Lamp, 1960. Design by Verner Panton, www.verner-panton.com © Verner Panton Design AG

Original promotional image of the Big Mushroom Chair, designed by Pierre Paulin for Artifort in 1960

Big Mushroom Chair, designed by Pierre Paulin for Artifort in 1960
Tulip Midi Chair, designed by Pierre Paulin for Artifort in 1960

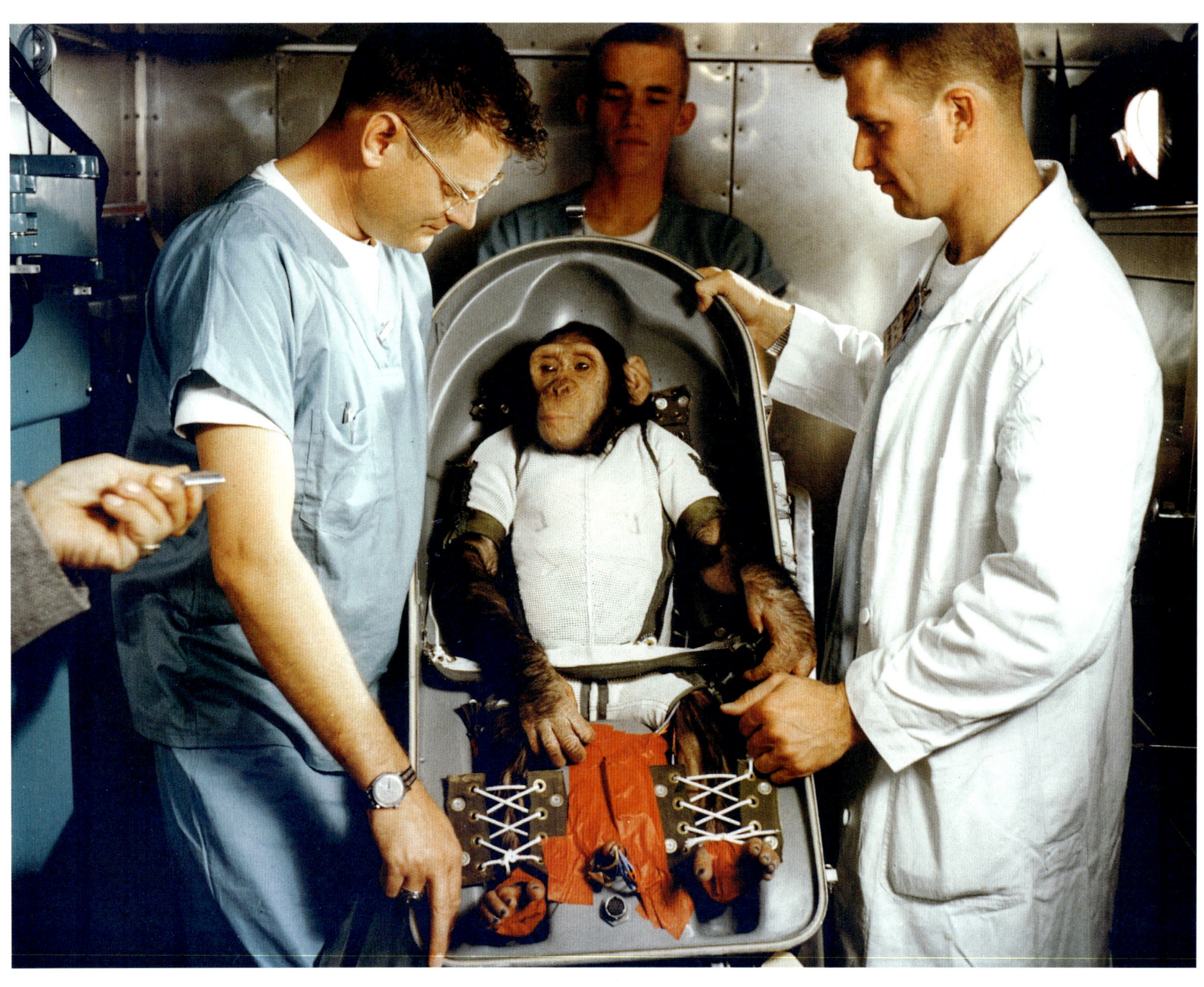

Ham, a three-year-old chimpanzee, preparing for the Mercury-Redstone 2 mission, where he became the first great ape launched into space, January 1961

Project Mercury astronaut Donald Slayton training on an air-bearing orbital attitude simulator at Langley Air Force base circa 1959. The extreme and exotic training program the Mercury Seven astronauts underwent was a great source of fascination to the American public, and one which NASA harnessed to keep the public onside

1956 print advertisement by Herbert Matter for Knoll's Tulip Chair, designed by Eero Saarinen in 1955–56

Eero Saarinen's Pedestal (or "Tulip") series are a seminal piece of sculptural design from the Space-Age era. Considered at the time a marker of cultural savviness and sophistication, they have remained so, becoming iconic pieces that are still manufactured by Knoll today. The architect and author Donald Albrecht says: "Saarinen's furnishings were his buildings in miniature."

Dining room of the Miller House in Indiana by architect and designer Eero Saarinen, completed in 1957, featuring Saarinen's Tulip Chairs

Early-1960s advertisement for the Knoll Associates Pedestal Chair, designed by Eero Saarinen in 1955–56

Launch of the Mercury Atlas, an unmanned suborbital Mercury capsule test, February 1961

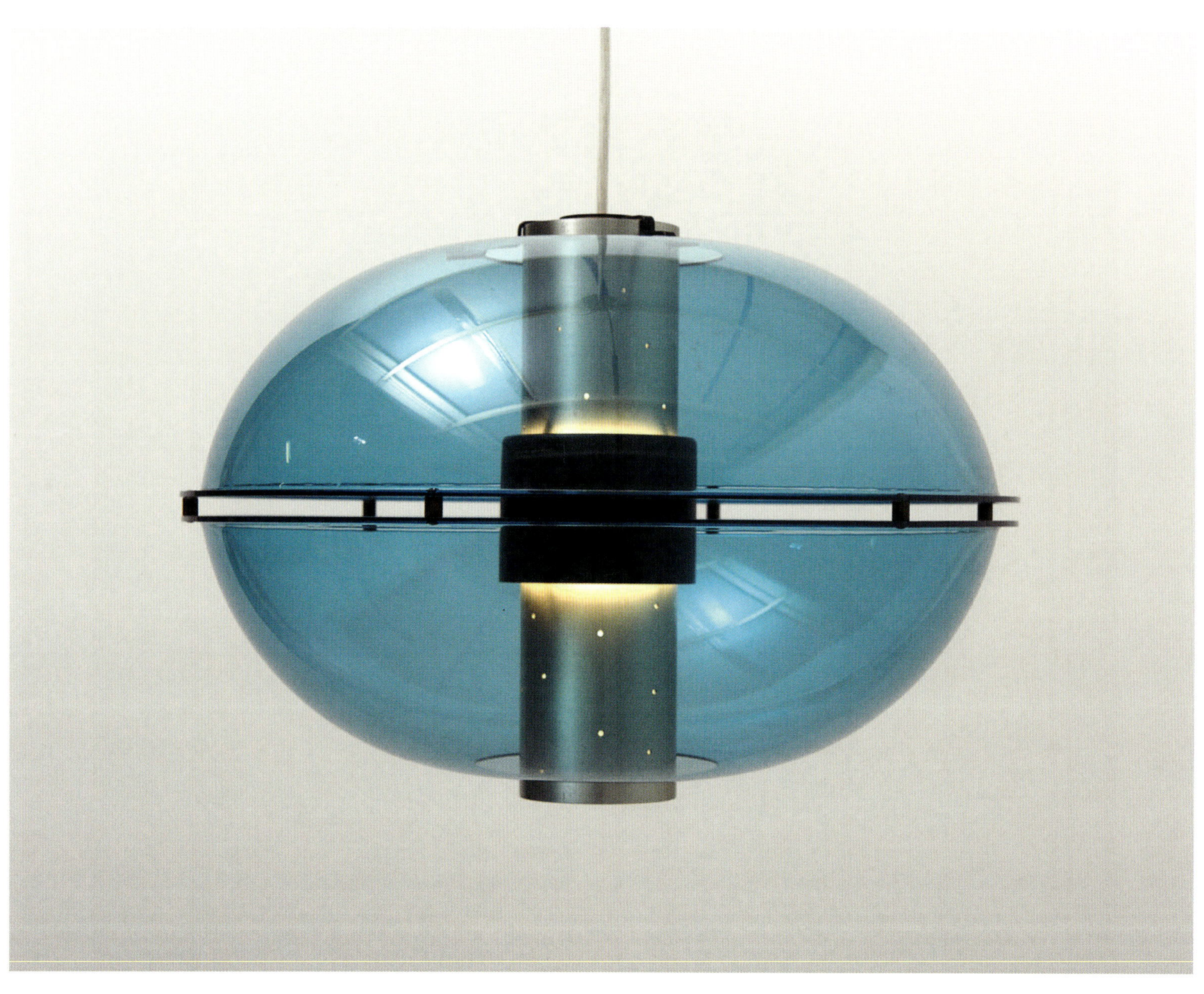

Orbiter acrylic pendant lampshade made by RAAK, c. 1960 (courtesy Modest Furniture)

NASA researchers analyze a moon dust simulation, 1960

Space-Age 3751 Plexi Table Lamp, early 1960s (courtesy Modest Furniture)

Verner Panton Hive Pendant Light, 1960 Design by Verner Panton / © Verner Panton Design AG & Verpan A/S

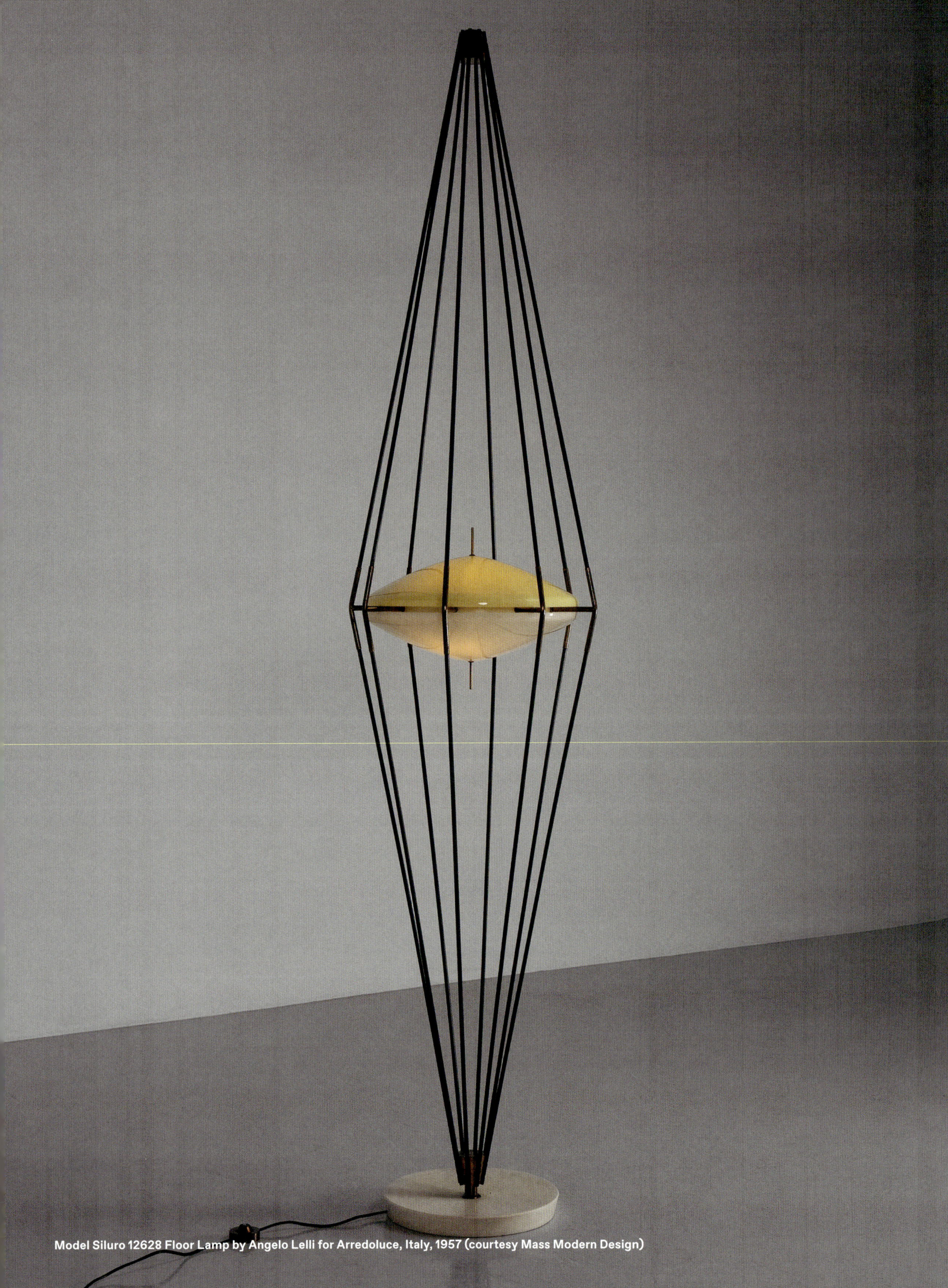

Model Siluro 12628 Floor Lamp by Angelo Lelli for Arredoluce, Italy, 1957 (courtesy Mass Modern Design)

NACA test pilot George Cooper at Ames Research Center, 1957

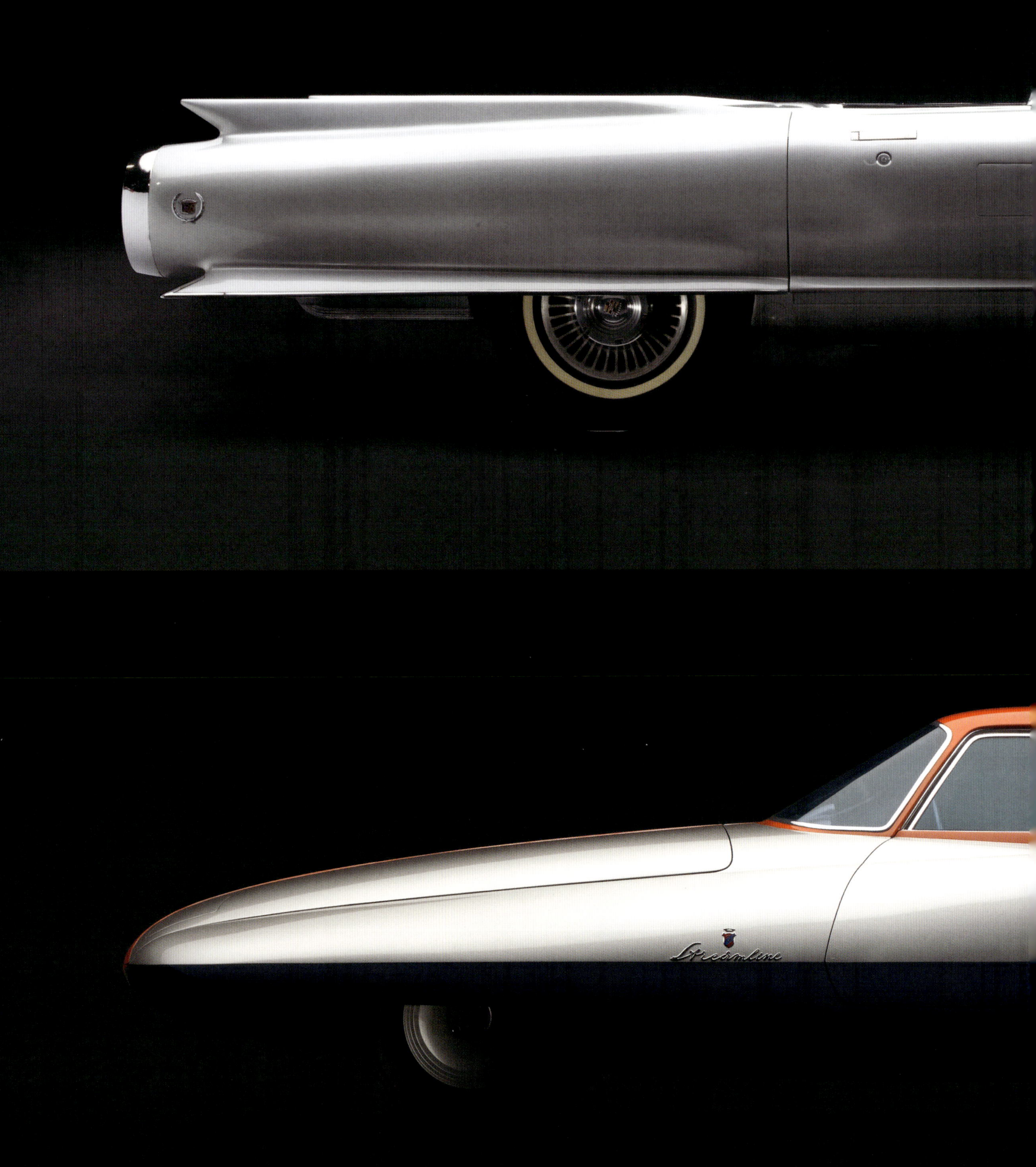

The era when cars went Space-Age: (top) Cadillac Cyclone XP-74, 1959 (bottom) Chrysler Ghia Gilda, 1955

1959 Cadillac Eldorado Biarritz Convertible

1958 General Motors Firebird III Concept Vehicle

L. Gordon Cooper, Jr., one of the original Mercury Seven astronauts, 1959

Verner Panton Moon Pendant, 1960 Design by Verner Panton / © Verner Panton Design AG & Verpan A/S

FRENZY 1961–1968

PART II

“Sputnik gave birth to NASA and Gagarin’s flight gave birth to Apollo.”

John Logsdon, professor emeritus at George Washington University’s Space Policy Institute

In 1961, America was losing the space race. The Soviet Union had achieved a run of dazzling firsts—first satellite, first animal in space, first lunar fly-past; and now, the one that would be remembered forever: Gagarin, the first human in space. “Sputnik might have shocked the world,” says Teasel Muir-Harmony, curator of the Project Apollo collection at the Smithsonian National Air and Space Museum, “but Gagarin’s flight impressed them. And that was even more politically troubling for the United States.”

Kennedy was in the White House when Gagarin went into orbit. But he was only a few months into the job, so any perceived failings of the American space program to date were clearly on the outgoing Eisenhower administration. Eisenhower—stung by repeated media and Democrat accusations of having been asleep at the wheel—had attempted to frame space exploration not as a competition, but as a scientific endeavor. The U.S. space program, so this narrative went, was about making life better for everyone on Earth, whereas the Soviets were indulging in performative demonstrations—showy space spectaculars and firsts.

This argument was particularly aimed at an international audience. “They were trying to differentiate the U.S. space program from the Soviet Union’s, and by extension, the U.S. political system from the Soviet system,” says Muir-Harmony, to demonstrate how “the United States was an open democratic society—and open about their space program in contrast to the secrecy surrounding the Soviet program.”

This is because in 1961, prestige mattered. The Cold War had framed the world order as an existential conflict between the free world and Soviet totalitarianism. And with almost 40 newly independent countries appearing in Africa and Asia between the end of the war and Kennedy’s inauguration, this battle for global influence, in the era of the domino theory, was seen as critical. For the USSR to be perceived as an advanced, world-leading country was to cede many of these potential nascent democracies and allies to the Soviet sphere.

This created a tension between Kennedy, who needed dramatic results to match and ideally beat the Soviets, and NASA, who had a long-term plan, designed in 1959, that they wanted to stick to. “It was designed by engineers—you can tell that immediately,” says Roger D. Launius, his point being that it wasn’t a political plan—it was a stepwise, logical program to achieve not public-relations triumphs but open-ended, long-term goals, and it ran like this: 1: Put someone in orbit to see if humans can survive up there. 2: Build a winged reusable vehicle that makes it easy to go to and from space. 3: Build a space station, which the winged reusable vehicle will service. 4: Use that space station as a jumping-off point to go to the moon, and then 5: Onwards to Mars.

This is not what happened. Instead, on 25 May 1961, just a few months into the job and four months after Gagarin’s triumph, Kennedy stepped up to the podium in Congress and announced: “I believe that this nation should commit itself to achieving the goal, before this decade is out, of landing a man on the moon and returning him safely to the Earth. No single space project in this period will be more impressive to mankind, or more important for the long-range exploration of space; and none will be so difficult or expensive to accomplish.” Kennedy, bold, shrewd, and intensely attuned to the exigencies of the Cold War, had ripped up NASA’s plan and was betting the farm on an American space triumph that would, if successful, define an era and provide a mortal blow to Soviet prestige.

“I believe that this nation should commit itself to achieving the goal, before this decade is out, of landing a man on the moon and returning him safely to the Earth.”

ARCHITECTURE

In March 1962, a month after John Glenn had become the first American to orbit Earth as part of the Mercury program, Eero Saarinen's Space-Age TWA Flight Center opened in New York. Described by the architect and author Donald Albrecht as "a modern-day Statue of Liberty that welcomed people to America's financial and cultural capital," it was a palace of soaring, Space-Age design emblematic of the confidence that characterized America at that moment. From the outside, two vast wings seem poised to take off. The inside was a cathedral of concrete, tubes, sinuous curves, and exotic futurism.

The TWA Flight Center operated as terminal until 2001; it has now been fully restored and repurposed as the TWA Hotel, with all the original 1962 styling and Space-Age furniture, especially Saarinen's Tulip tables and chairs.

When Saarinen began work on Flight Center in 1956, he was already one of America's best-known architects. His use of technical innovations such as Cor-ten steel and mirrored glass had generated enormous press, as had breathtakingly futuristic structures such as the polished steel sculptural water tower at the General Motors Technical Center (1956), and his Gateway Arch in St Louis, described by Albrecht as a "monumental portal leading to Jefferson's Louisiana Purchase, west of the Mississippi River." These, together with TWA Flight Center, form some of the bravest and most forward-looking architectural legacies of the Space-Age era.

Another now-iconic example of exuberant Space-Age airport design is the Theme Building at Los Angeles International Airport, built between 1957 and 1961. It's an "enigmatic concrete spaceship," according to *Architecture Today*, "a monument to Tinseltown's Swinging 60s glamour, and to the lost opportunities of the American Space Age." L.A. in the 1950s and 60s was not short of space-inspired architecture; what's notable is the caliber of the architects executing it. John Lautner's 1960 Chemosphere house in Los Angeles looks like a UFO perched over a cliff and was described by *Encyclopædia Britannica* as "the most modern home built in the world." Lautner's dazzling Arthur Elrod House in Palm Springs, with its circular concrete roof and panoramic glazing, is pure Bond-villain—and it did actually feature in the Bond film *Diamonds Are Forever*.

As the mid-1960s began to unfold, space influence began its zenith, a giddy climb that would take the world to the moon landings; and as the Mercury Program, and then Gemini, and then Apollo, played out, and with Soviet successes ranging from Mars flypasts to space walks, space became one of the principal canvases against which global culture played out.

TELSTAR

In December 1962, a strange, reedy, unsettling sound began emitting from transistor radios across the world. It was a clavioline—a weird-sounding forerunner of the synthesizer, and the song was an eerie, anthemic mash-up of sci-fi overlaid with the kind of frontier grandeur evoked by golden-age Western movie soundtracks of the 1950s and 60s.

There are certain times when a record lands in such a way and at such a time that it encapsulates the spirit of a moment, and that's what happened to the British band The Tornadoes with their song *Telstar*. Named after the experimental Telstar communications satellite that had launched a few months earlier from Cape Canaveral, it had reached the top of the charts in the U.S., the UK, and Canada by 1963, and the top 10 in many other countries including West Germany and Australia, selling millions of copies worldwide. A British band at No. 1 in the U.S. was not a normal event in 1963—this was pre-the Beatles, pre-British Invasion, and it was the first time it had happened.

PANTON CHAIR

1963 is also when Verner Panton first started collaborating with Swiss furniture company Vitra on what was to become known as the Panton Chair.

Originally conceived in 1959, the Panton Chair was, and remains, a genuine global cover star. One of the most photographed chairs of the 1960s, dazzling in its bold, saturated colors, and with a sensuous sheen and sinuous litheness, it has a sculptural visual simplicity that has been beguiling people since its prototype was first spotted in Panton's studio by Rolf Fehlbaum, son of Vitra's founders, Willi and Erika Fehlbaum. The world's first stackable, single-material, injection-molded chair, it appears, in the words of Vitra's classics design manager Stine Liv Buur, as "more a frozen movement than an object."

Buur goes on to say: "The Panton Chair is one of the most important chairs of the 20th century. It's an icon: its shape is recognized by most people, and its design has become better known than the designer himself or its producer, Vitra, for that matter."

Verner Panton's daughter Carin Panton von Halem says: "I realize that I am biased in this matter, but I believe that even today, the Panton chair is one of the most beautiful chairs ever made—and its success clearly proves my claim, as many other people seem to think so too. I believe the enduring success of this chair is significantly linked to its extravagant appearance and sculptural quality. Once you have seen it, you will never forget it."

The story of the Panton Chair is the story of design in the Space Age era writ large. It's the story of experimentation, audacity, and a singularity of vision enabled by collaboration with manufacturers. It's the story of materiality, tireless iteration, frustration, and ultimate success. Like many creative endeavors, making something look simple and effortless can be complex and difficult; and executing Panton's cantilever chair took decades to perfect. Liv Buur describes the early years of Verner Panton's and Vitra's work on the chair: "It turned out to be a nearly impossible challenge, as the bold contours imagined by the designer had to be reconciled with the physical limits of plastics technology and manufacturing requirements at the time." She adds: "It involved several years of research, testing, discarded designs and continuous prototype development: the final shape of the chair was the culmination of 10 prototypes made of manually laminated, glass-fiber-reinforced polyester."

It wasn't until 1967 that Panton Chair was unveiled for the first time in Danish design journal *Mobilia*. The limited pilot edition of just 150 pieces made an immediate impact on the design world. Serial production began a year later using rigid polyurethane foam from Bayer. In the 1990s when the plastic industry had further developed, Verner Panton and Vitra reprised the project in order to create a more affordable version of the classic Panton Chair. Panton was closely involved in the project and managed to approve the final product, but sadly died just before this new stackable version joined the Panton Chair Classic on the market in 1999.

"The whole Space-Age aesthetic goes very much hand-in-hand with plastic," says Johanna Agerman Ross, chief curator at the London Design Museum. "And the Panton chair is probably the pinnacle."

"The Panton Chair is one of the most important chairs of the 20th century. It's an icon: its shape is recognized by most people, and its design has become better known than the designer himself or its producer, Vitra, for that matter."

THE GEMINI PROGRAM

With NASA's long-term plan for space exploration now diverted into Kennedy's all-out dash for the moon, NASA needed a rethink. Apollo—and the Saturn V rocket that would power it—was already in planning but years away from being realized. And while the Mercury program had fulfilled its objective of getting a person into space and back again, it was limited. "The Mercury capsule could operate for a few hours—I think the last mission was 36 hours—and that was about the extent of its capabilities," says Launius. "You couldn't maneuver the capsule much, and you couldn't get out of it."

Gemini provided the technical bridge between what had already been achieved with Mercury, and what would be needed for the Apollo program to succeed. "Gemini allowed the U.S. to learn how to rendezvous and dock in space, how to fly missions long enough to get to the moon, how to create fuel cells that were needed for such long missions, and many other things," says former NASA chief historian William P. Barry. "It also trained NASA—mission controllers, astronauts, and everyone else—on how to run a space program while waiting for the Saturn V rocket and Apollo spacecraft to be built."

VALENTINA TERESHKOVA

NASA was making solid progress with Project Gemini, but the plan wouldn't involve any crewed missions until 1965. And meanwhile, the Soviet Union kept scoring firsts.

On 16 June 1963, Soviet cosmonaut Valentina Tereshkova became the first woman in space, spending nearly three days in orbit in Vostok 6. It was another Soviet public relations coup, but tragically, that's all it turned out to be. While the Soviet Union made much of its equality between the sexes—and with women having fought alongside men in the Second World War—it was not matched by action, at least in space. Having scored the first, the Soviets quietly dropped the female cosmonaut program, such as it had even existed; and it would not be until 1982 that another female cosmonaut would fly.

It was no better in the United States. Tereshkova had racked up more space hours in one mission than the combined total achieved by all the male American astronauts by 1963, yet women—while out-performing men in data points across the space training program—would be blocked from the opportunity of becoming astronauts until Sally Ride's Space Shuttle mission in 1983.

And in 1964, with the Americans focusing on Project Gemini, the Soviets scored yet another first with a fly-past of Mars.

OLIVIER MOURGUE'S DJINN

In the same year, the futuristic Djinn Chaise Longue by French industrial designer Olivier Mourgue was unveiled—part of a series manufactured by Airborne that included a chair and a two-seater sofa. Now in the permanent collections of museums across the world including New York's MoMA and MET and London's V&A, the Djinn's low-slung, almost gelatinous appearance—formed from wool jersey stretched over sculpted polyurethane on a steel-tube frame—made them instantly visually appealing and, together with their saturated monoblock colors, have made them an enduring Space-Age design classic. They also owe a part of their iconic stature to their famous appearance in Stanley Kubrick's 1968 film *2001: A Space*

Odyssey—where they furnish the Hilton hotel lobby of Space Station Five. It might be a niche category, but it's not hyperbolic to describe Olivier Mourgue's Djinn as the most famous screen-chair of the 20th century.

SPACEWALK

In 1965, an event happened that dramatically marked a point of divergence between the natures of the American and Soviet space programs. But while in retrospect it reveals a watershed, that's not how it looked at the time.

Early on the morning of 18 March, Soviet cosmonaut Alexei Leonov climbed out of the narrow porthole on the Voskhod Space Capsule, piloted by Pavel Belyayev, and performed the first-ever spacewalk. In keeping with the Soviet policy of secrecy, nothing had been announced beforehand; his father, watching a live feed on the ground, shouted at the screen: "Why is he acting like a juvenile delinquent? What is he doing clambering about outside?"

But the spacewalk had, of course, been planned, and the timing was no accident. In the United States, the Gemini program had scheduled a spacewalk by Ed White in June that year. And in contrast to the covert nature of the Soviet program, NASA had openly published their timetable—giving the Soviets an opportunity to pip their rivals again with another major first.

Things, however, didn't go to plan. No longer constricted by the claustrophobic spacecraft, Leonov's suit began to balloon alarmingly. While Soviet premier Brezhnev sat watching the live feed with members of the Politburo, Leonov pulled himself back to the airlock, but realized he couldn't re-enter—the deformed and expanded space suit was now too big to fit through the narrow aperture.

In desperation, the cosmonaut spun around and tried again, head-first. But the suit was too stiff; he still couldn't fit. So, hundreds of miles above Earth and hurtling through space at thousands of miles an hour, Leonov grasped the valve in the lining of his suit and bled some of the high-pressure oxygen out of it. As he grappled with the airlock, the temperature started rising dangerously high. Sweat sloshed around inside his suit as he began to get the bends from the decompression.

Leonov eventually made it back into the capsule alive. But re-entry into Earth's atmosphere was terrifying: the automatic guidance system malfunctioned, and they had to land manually; a tailspin put them into a colossal 10G, bursting the blood vessels in their eyes. They overshot the landing zone by almost 1,000 miles (1,600km).

Leonov's story illustrates many things. It demonstrates that space travel was still extremely hazardous. It demonstrates how important the propaganda value of trumping the Americans in space landmarks remained. But it also delineates a high-water mark of these achievements, and the borderline recklessness with which the Soviets chased them, in contrast to the step-by-step approach of the Gemini program, which hadn't yet borne such flashy results, but soon would.

"Leonov lived a long time, well past the Soviet era, and he never stopped talking about all the crazy crap they did," says Launius. "He almost died—it was a poorly executed plan, just to beat the Americans. How foolhardy that was, quite frankly."

EERO AARNIO'S BALL CHAIR

In January 1966, a chair that the *New York Times* described as "three-quarters of a fresh orange" debuted at the Cologne Furniture Fair. If one had to select the chair that most encapsulates the 1960s, many would choose the Ball Chair by Finnish designer Eero Aarnio. 1960s icons Nancy Sinatra, Françoise Hardy, and the Small Faces were photographed in it. The V&A museum places it at the top of their list of Space-Age chairs, and they go on to say: "Pod-like furniture designs recurred throughout the 1960s, inspired by space capsules and the idea of futuristic cities populated by 'pod-like' dwellings. Eero Aarnio's Ball Chair became an icon of pop design, with its distinctly unnatural space-capsule-like character."

Eero Aarnio himself says: "I believe that I designed the Ball Chair at the right time. The world was ready for a new look in furniture in the 1960s. It was a good time to launch fresh ideas in furniture design; to use bright colors, round and organic forms, and the use of new materials such as fiberglass and plastic in furniture manufacturing helped designers to move away from the more traditional shapes. When the Ball Chair was launched in the 1966 Cologne Furniture Fair, it caused a sensation and was sold in 30 countries in one week."

Aarnio designed many further pieces during the Space-Age era that are recognizable throughout the world today, including the Pastil (1967), the Bubble Chair (1968), and the Tomato (1971). And he's still designing relevant work today, in his 90s. But it's the Ball Chair that nailed the preoccupations and needs of an era; it's still a favorite of AD100 interior designers, who use it to add flavor and attitude to upscale projects, and it will not be going away any time soon.

"Eero Aarnio's Ball Chair became an icon of pop design, with its distinctly unnatural space-capsule-like character."

SERGEI KOROLEV

The Cologne fair where Aarnio's chair caused such a sensation came just three weeks after the death of one of the towering figures of the space race: the chief engineer of the Soviet space program, Sergei Korolev. Ask many senior NASA personnel to name figures of the era they respect, and Korolev is usually on their list.

Korolev's is a very Soviet story. Born in 1907 in Ukraine, his father was Russian-Belorussian and his mother Ukrainian-Polish-Greek. First a pilot, later a rocket engineer, he became a key member of the Reactive Scientific Research Institute, which brought together the best of the Soviet rocket talent including Valentin Glushko—another central figure in the Soviet space effort. In his purge of intellectuals, Stalin in 1937 had Korolev arrested, tortured, and sent off to a brutal Siberian gulag. It nearly killed him; the once-handsome engineer had a heart attack and lost most of his teeth from beatings and scurvy (years later, he sent Gagarin into space with the benediction: "Come back with all your teeth, Yuri.").

At war and desperate for engineers, Stalin recalled Korolev in 1940, where he rejoined the rocket program—from jail. On his release in 1945, he was sent off to Germany: Just as the Americans had scooped up Wernher von Braun and his team of V2 rocket engineers, the Soviets had captured Nazi stores of V2 rocket components and needed someone who understood them.

At the time of his death in 1966, the whole world knew Gagarin, but almost no one outside the immediate classified circle of the Soviet space program had heard of Korolev. Yet almost alone, Korolev had created the ability to beat the United States in sending a man into orbit. One of the things that has emerged through the years is quite what a shoestring operation the Soviet space program was, and quite how hairy so many of their missions were. It took a man with Korolev's force of personality to hold it together. "Sergei Korolev was, initially, the genius behind the Soviet space program and the architect of all of those space firsts that they chalked up in the late 1950s to early 1960s," says Barry. "He knew how to make the Soviet system work, had a keen eye for talent, knew how to lead, and was a fearless risk-taker... While the U.S. had half a dozen different space boosters, the Soviets made all of their early accomplishments with just one rocket. I still find it quite remarkable."

PIERRE PAULIN

In 1966, shortly after the Soviets had buried Korolev, French furniture manufacturer Artifort introduced a lithe, otherworldly chair in a startling chromatic powder blue—the Ribbon Chair. Its creator was a young French designer, Pierre Paulin.

Years later, French President Nicolas Sarkozy would pay tribute to him as "the man who made design an art." In the same way that it took Daft Punk to recontextualize disco in the early 2000s, it was to a large extent French collectors and gallerists in the 21st century who were the first to rediscover, define, and celebrate the idea of Space-Age design. This is partly because in Paulin, France had a totemic designer-artist whose sensuous, supersaturated chairs emphatically recalibrated the era's aesthetics. They bequeathed to the design world a vivid, sophisticated hinterland that continues to exert influence—it's notable, for example, that his rediscovered prototypes, now created as limited editions by his family's studio Paulin Paulin Paulin, are one of the must-see installations at Miami Art Week—itself the essential event on the global art and design calendar.

The Ribbon Chair joined a line-up of iconic pieces by Pierre Paulin that included the Mushroom (1958), Orange Slice (1960), Groovy Chair (1964), and Tulip (1965)—all of which were created during a long and successful partnership with Artifort, and nearly all of which are still in the manufacturer's current catalog.

Paulin was a big deal throughout the entire span of the Space Age era. In the 1970s, President Georges Pompidou commissioned him to design an installation at the Élysée Palace (the 'Paulin Room' is still there, created with the same cast aluminum and plastic coating as was used for the cabins of the Apollo spacecraft). And in the 1980s, François Mitterrand commissioned him to design his presidential office.

Benjamin Paulin, his son—and a partner of Paulin Paulin Paulin—describes how the Ribbon chair came to be. "My father was influenced by designers such as Charles and Ray Eames and Alvar Aalto. But he was also influenced by new techniques and new possibilities," he says. "He discovered that it was possible to use Bauhaus tubulars to make the structures, then to use Pirelli foam to create comfort and shape; and then to upholster using stretchy jersey material, making all the technical aspects disappear so that we are left with a pure, organic structure with no joints that you can see from any side—like a sculpture."

This is not entirely different from Olivier Mourgue's technique with the 1964 Djinn series. But Paulin was using this technique back in 1957, while designing the Mushroom chair; and it was a discovery that influenced designers including Verner Panton. Paulin perfected the concept through several further models, including the Dome chair and the Groovy chair, all of which used the tubular structure, molded foam, and stretchy fabric. "They are just functional shapes," says Benjamin Paulin of the seamless, sculptural forms that eschewed patterns and any notion of traditional details. "There is never any decorative intention."

This is partly why Paulin's work has a certain transfigurated quality, as if they have arrived from a different plane of existence. Benjamin Paulin gives a clue as to what gives them this sense of exceptionalism: "My father was fascinated with the prehistoric past, and with the future. Not so much by the present. His generation had witnessed the discovery of the prehistoric drawings of Lascaux, and they witnessed the discovery of space. It changed their lives. Those were very strong moments in his lifetime, and both were very influential on his work."

"My father was influenced by designers such as Charles and Ray Eames and Alvar Aalto. But he was also influenced by new techniques and new possibilities."

SPACE, CULTURE AND THE COUNTER-CULTURE

From the mid-1960s onwards, the world entered Peak Space Age. Project Gemini, developing capabilities for the upcoming Apollo program, flew 10 crewed missions in 1965 and 1966, and it grabbed a lot of attention. "The lack of significant Soviet human space flights and the pace of Gemini missions actually made it look like the U.S. had jumped into the lead in space," says Barry. Opinion polls from 1966 showed that the American public now believed they were edging ahead in the space race.

The riveting pace of progress continued to seep into the wider culture. *Star Trek* began broadcasting in 1966 and rapidly became a worldwide pop-culture sensation (it has since become one of the highest-grossing franchises of all time). Its success was both a reflection of the fascination with space in the global imagination and an agent for its propagation. It also played a role in the alignment of space exploration with the counterculture. This is a crucial reason why from the mid-1960s onwards, space was seen as progressive, sexy, and fashionable—all reasons why Space Age design has taken on a talismanic quality that has echoed down the decades.

But space was not the only live issue in the 1960s. For many people, it wasn't even the most important. Throughout 1960s America, civil rights were the defining issue of the decade. Then there was Vietnam, which itself was a corollary of the Cold War. The Berlin Wall had been built in 1961, a microcosm of sorts for the front-line atmosphere of Europe in the 1960s and 70s. France, having grappled with fallout from the Algerian War in the early 60s, was now grappling with internal unrest that would culminate in the riots of 1968.

The space race was not divorced from these realities. To return to *Star Trek*: the show, as well as contributing to the frenzy of interest in space exploration in the mid-60s onwards, also helped ally it with what then was called the counter-culture. Gene Roddenberry, creator of *Star Trek*, reputedly told friends he'd modeled it on *Gulliver's Travels*—with each episode working on two levels: the first as a gripping adventure story; the second as a morality tale. By creating, he said, a new world with new rules, "I could make statements about sex, religion, Vietnam, politics, and intercontinental missiles. Indeed, we did make them on *Star Trek*: we were sending messages and fortunately, they all got by the network."

More fundamentally, the American space race had been given a wide frame from the start. Lyndon Johnson had been in charge of the U.S. space program since the beginning of Kennedy's administration. With his experience of Roosevelt's New Deal in the 1930s and projects like the Tennessee Valley Authority, Johnson had seen the potential impact that such a vast civil project could have on American industry and life. "He thought this was a way to modernize the nation, and it would help address some of the racial issues the United States was grappling with, especially in the American South," says Muir-Harmony. "Johnson was able to sell it as a national project with international impact, but with domestic impact as well. And that's part of why he was able to get the congressional support to invest at the level of funding that was necessary for the Apollo program."

This sense of a grand national project for the good of the nation goes some way to explaining how the Gemini and Apollo programs energized the national mood to the extent that it did. If the space race had been perceived solely as a tool of the Cold War, it might not have changed the objective results, but it would have affected how it landed with the public. In the event, it permeated design, fashion, music, art, and film with very little of the cynicism that might meet such an undertaking now. The space race might have had politically motivated origins, but it was not solely seen that way—and where it was, it did not tarnish it. Instead, it remained gripping, aspirational, and fashionable for a generation.

And as the world embarked on enormous societal change, space exploration became an emblem of that change. The grand canvas of it—the incomprehensible vastness, the bravery, the frontier mentality—spoke to a sense of shared enterprise that, even as a vector of the Cold War, also managed to be a metaphor for how we could move beyond it.

Apollo 7 launch, Kennedy Space Center, October 1968

Aero Spacelines Pregnant Guppy, designed to transport the third stage of the Saturn V rocket, preparing for flight tests in 1962

Irvine and Estelle Laverne Champagne Chairs for Formes Nouvelles, 1962 (City Furniture)

Staircase in polyester foam, steel and lacquer, designed by Georges Ferran for Axe circa mid-1960s–1971 (Morentz)

Gemini-Titan spacecraft on the launch pad, 1964

(above) Ed White became the first American to conduct a spacewalk during the Gemini 4 mission in June 1965.
(right) TV designed by Verner Panton for Wega-Radio, 1963. Design by Verner Panton, www.verner-panton.com © Verner Panton Design AG

Astronaut Virgil I. Grissom, command pilot of the Gemini-Titan 3 (GT-3) space flight, March 1965

Donyale Luna modelling Paco Rabanne's iconic Space Age Dress, photographed by Guy Bourdin for *Vogue*, 1966

NASA test for the Gemini Spacesuit, January 1966

Test engineers fire up the Saturn I rocket's first stage at the Propulsion and Structural Test Facility at NASA's Marshall Space Flight Center, 1964

Soviet Propaganda Poster: “Soviet Man Be Proud, You Opened the Way to the Stars”, 1963

Apollo mission test: Launch of the Little Joe II rocket, carrying a scale model of the launch escape system.
White Sands Missile Range, New Mexico, August 1963

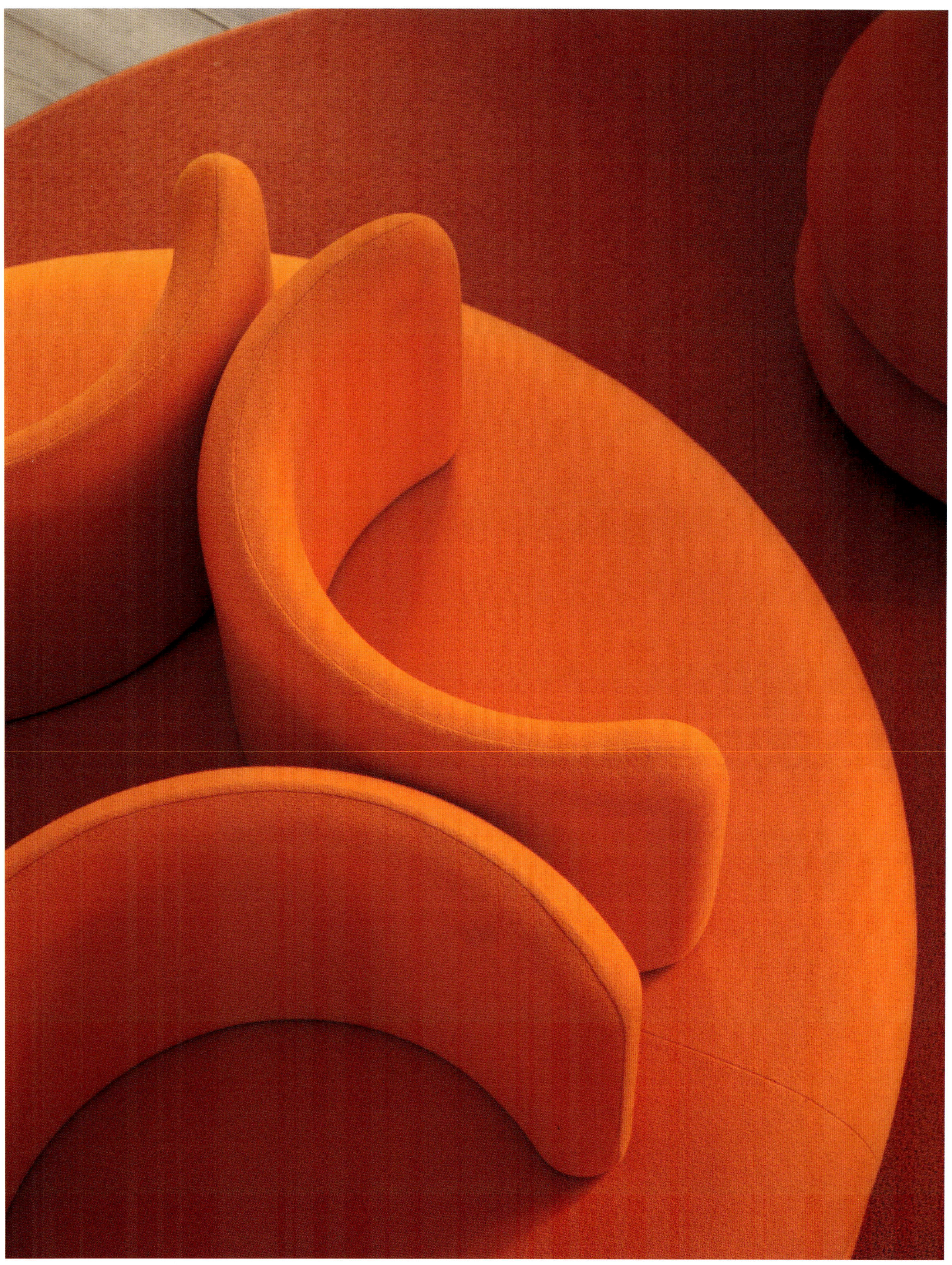

Easy Sofa, design by Verner Panton / © Verner Panton Design AG & Verpan A/S 1963

Easy Chair, design by Verner Panton / © Verner Panton Design AG & Verpan A/S 1963

Easy Chair, design by Verner Panton / © Verner Panton Design AG & Verpan A/S 1963

Easy Sofa, design by Verner Panton / © Verner Panton Design AG & Verpan A/S 1963

Eero Aarnio sitting inside in his iconic Ball Chair, designed in 1963 and produced from 1965

Two icons from the 1960s: (left) Eero Aarnio's Ball Chair is almost visual shorthand for the era, so perfectly did it capture the zeitgeist. Aarnio, still designing well into his 90s, tells us: "I believe that I designed the Ball Chair at the right time. The world was ready for a new look in furniture in the 1960s." When the Ball Chair was launched in the 1966 Cologne Furniture Fair, it caused a sensation and was sold in 30 countries in one week.

Another icon—and one that spawned Number 1 records in the U.S. and UK—is the experimental Telstar communications satellite, which provided the first live transatlantic TV and telephone relay through space.

Telstar communications satellite, launched July 1962 (Model at Conservatoire National des Arts et Métiers, Paris)

NASA test subject equipped with Gemini 12 Life Support System for extravehicular activity (space-walking) 1966

Eero Aarnio Ball Chair, mid-1960s

Verner Panton landscaped interior for A. Kill/ Metzeler Schaum, 1965–67
Design by Verner Panton, www.verner-panton.com © Verner Panton Design AG

Eero Saarinen's Saint Louis Gateway Arch, 1965

Lunar Landing Research Vehicle, NASA Flight Research Center, 1967

The sculptural Panton Chair is a genuine global cover star and one of the most photographed chairs of the 1960s, dazzling in its bold, saturated colors, and with a sensuous sheen and sinuous litheness. It appears, in the words of Vitra's classics design manager Stine Liv Buur, as "more a frozen movement than an object." Johanna Agerman Ross, chief curator at the London Design Museum, says: "The whole Space-Age aesthetic goes very much hand-in-hand with plastic. And the Panton chair is probably the pinnacle."

Panton Chair Classic from Vitra, designed in 1958 by Verner Panton and manufactured from 1967

NASA engineer Bobby Sanders watches as a scale model of the Apollo Command Module is prepared for dynamic stability tests in a supersonic wind tunnel, 1964

Pierre Paulin Groovy Chair for Artifort, 1964 (courtesy Modest Furniture)

Malitte by Roberto Matta (Paradisoterrestre Edition), 1966

Djinn Chair 7000 Rose 2 (Japanese Advertisement), designed by Olivier Mourgue for Airborne, 1965
Olivier Mourgue Chaise Lounge for Airborne, 1965

The futuristic Djinn Chair and Chaise Longue by French industrial designer Olivier Mourgue were unveiled in 1964, manufactured by Airborne. Now in the permanent collections of New York's MoMA and MET and London's V&A, the Djinn's low-slung appearance made it instantly visually appealing. It also owes part of its iconic stature to its famous appearance in Stanley Kubrick's 1968 film *2001: A Space Odyssey,* where they furnish the Hilton hotel lobby of Space Station Five.

Pair of Djinn Easy Chairs (courtesy of Modest Furniture), designed by Olivier Mourgue in 1965
Djinn chairs seen in Stanley Kubrick's 1968 film *2001: A Space Odyssey*

Unmanned Saturn V launch for the Apollo 6 mission,
lifting off from the Kennedy Space Center launch complex in April 1968

Françoise Hardy wearing Paco Rabanne's gold and diamond Space Age dress, Paris, 1968

The expended Saturn S-IVB stage, photographed from the Apollo 7 spacecraft at an approximate altitude of 125 nautical miles, October 1968

Verner Panton: Multi-functional living unit, 1966 Design by Verner Panton, www.verner-panton.com © Verner Panton Design AG

F585 Lounge Chair by Geoffrey D. Harcourt for Artifort in 1967

Archive promotional image, Geoffrey D. Harcourt Lounge Chair for Artifort, 1967

(left) Verner Panton landscaped interior for the Visiona 0 exhibition in 1968. Design by Verner Panton, www.verner-panton.com © Verner Panton.
(above) The radio systems of an Apollo spacecraft being tested in an anechoic chamber designed to simulate the echo-free depths of space, 1967

The iconic 'Earthrise' image, taken aboard Apollo 8 by Bill Anders during the first crewed spacecraft circumnavigation of the moon, December 1968

Acrylic Sphere 'Apollo 12' by Danilo Silvestrin, 1968

Alvar lounge chair and ottoman by Giuseppe Raimondi for Gufram, 1966

Karelia by Lisii Beckmann, designed for Zanotta in 1966

NASA astronaut Ed White, pilot on Gemini-Titan 4, during a spacewalk, June 1965

View of the orbiting Gemini 7 spacecraft taken from the Gemini 6 spacecraft during their rendezvous mission, December 1965

Tulip Chair by Pierre Paulin for Artifort, 1965

Lunar Landing Research Vehicle with Bell 47 helicopter providing chase support, 1965

Joe Colombo Elda Lounge Chair, 1963 (Kooloo Modern)

Bubble Chair by Christian Daninos for Laroche, 1968 (City Furniture)

Apollo 1 crew during water egress training, June 1966

1966 Eero Aarnio Pastil Chair, 1967

Blow by Jonathan De Pas, Donato D'Urbino and Paolo Lomazzi (with Scolari) for Zanotta, 1967

Designed by Jonathan De Pas, Donato D'Urbino and Paolo Lomazzi with Carla Scolari in 1967, the Blow chair was the first industrially produced and commercially successful inflatable chair, receiving an enthusiastic welcome when debuting at the Milan Furniture Fair the following year. "The Blow reflected a changing lifestyle—revolutionary ideas of an informal, flexible and dynamic house had swept away traditional ideas of domesticity," says Vitra Design Musem, adding that it "perfectly embodies the spirit of that time and therefore became an icon of the 1960s."

Earth photographed from Apollo 7, 1968

Pierre Paulin Dos à Dos / Face à Face, 1967

Eero Aarnio Bubble Chair, 1968

Entire western hemisphere visible from Apollo 8 spacecraft, 1968

Ligne Roset Asmara, 1968

THE APOLLO YEARS 1968–1972

PART III

The character of the 1960s had changed by the time of Apollo 1. A decade that had begun with Percy Faith now had The Doors. The Beatles had turned psychedelic. Protest movements grew. Vietnam was mired in despair. Interiors were more worldly, outré, and color-drenched. Fashion was Space-Age and metallic.

Apollo 1 is remembered now not as a new beginning but as an awful tragedy. On 27 January 1967, Gus Grissom, Ed White, and Roger B. Chaffee climbed into the Apollo command module to undertake a launch rehearsal for their inaugural mission. Clad in their nylon space suits, the three astronauts strapped into their launch positions and began their prelaunch checks while the cabin was pumped with pure oxygen, its high pressure tightly sealing the hatch from the atmosphere outside.

Then came one of the greatest disasters of the space race. Somehow, a spark issued from the yards of electrical wiring in the capsule. It ignited the pure oxygen cabin atmosphere as easily as a flame to a gas fire. The synthetic space suits combusted. All three astronauts died. Later, it would take a full five minutes for emergency workers to cut through the hatch.

The Apollo 1 tragedy set the program's timetable back by 20 months; no American crewed missions would fly until Apollo 7 in October 1968. During the hiatus, the Soviets would rack up yet more firsts.

In October 1967, the Soviet spacecraft Venera 4 reached Venus and analyzed its atmosphere—an extraordinary achievement just a decade after Sputnik. And in September 1968, Zond 5 performed the first return of a spacecraft to Earth after circling the moon.

And yet, for all their impressive firsts, the Soviet space program lacked the focus of a single objective. And Apollo 8, scheduled to launch in December 1968, was about to blow every prior achievement away.

SPACE-AGE FASHION

By 1968, Space-Age design was in the ascendency. Reflecting the intense fascination and romantic appeal of space exploration, fashion had embraced space as the epoch-defining issue and translated it into the aesthetic of the era. "The space race in the 1960s produced a crop of young designers aiming to equip the fashion masses for what they assumed to be the next frontier," says Lilah Ramzi in *American Vogue*. "Chin-strap space bonnets, flat ankle boots, and sleek, plastic-like tech fabrics typified the Space-Age look as women readied themselves for a new sartorial stratosphere."

French designer André Courrèges had launched his *Space Age* collection back in 1964, projecting a futuristic aesthetic with what Dominic Lutyens, writing in *BBC Style*, describes as "astronaut-like models attired in helmets, opaque sunglasses, and silver trousers."

British Vogue says: "He also helped to popularize other items that came to define the 'Moon Girl' look, including flat boots, goggles and trouser suits."

French designer Pierre Cardin championed the Space-Age aesthetic of silver vinyl at Paris Fashion Week in 1968. *CNN Style* describes Cardin as "a pioneer of Space-Age fashion, crafting sharp, modernist silhouettes from shimmering lamé fabric."

But if there's a single image that nails the futuristic élan of the late-1960s, it's that of French singer, model, and icon Françoise Hardy wearing Paco Rabanne's now-famous gold chain-mail dress. "In the hands of Spanish designer Paco Rabanne, the Space Race became the perfect stimulus for envisioning an avant-garde future," says *Vogue*.

His *Gold Rhodoid* dress as worn by the supermodel Donyale Luna and his dress for Jane Fonda in *Barbarella* are classics of the era. But it is Hardy's dress, which weighed 20 pounds (9kg), contained 1,000 gold plaques, and over 300 carats of diamonds, that—in the words of the *New York Times*—"changed the definition of couture".

"The space race in the 1960s produced a crop of young designers aiming to equip the fashion masses for what they assumed to be the next frontier."

COLOR

If fashion was mining white, silver, and gold, furniture design was embracing a kaleidoscope of saturated technicolor.

The relationship between furniture, color, and the democratization of design is central to the whole ethos of Space-Age design; and again, the Eames were pioneers in its use. "The Eames were clever in applying different types of color to the fiberglass chair," says the London Design Museum's Johanna Agerman Ross, "because it creates an opportunity to appeal to a broader audience and to fit many different contexts—whereas if you have a chair in wood, it's more dependent on what's around it. The colorfulness—and options for color—of these pieces was a big factor. It was also a great marketing tool for the plastics industry: it doesn't come in just one color, but whatever color you want."

For Cristina Bargna of Design Museum Brussels, color represented liberty. "There was the idea that after the war, we wanted to rebuild a new world. And this could be made with color and with lightness. Anyone could choose the color or shape."

The era's designer most closely associated with color was, of course, Verner Panton. "Colors meant everything to Verner Panton," says Vitra's Stine Liv Buur, "and he understood exactly how the nuances of different hues affect people's moods and the ambience of specific spaces."

Panton's daughter Carin Panton von Halem agrees. "My father loved colors," she says. "His intensive studies of color psychology made him aware of the effect of colors on our well-being—he saw color as part of the joy of living, and he was convinced that colors could improve our quality of life."

It's important to remember how the use of extensive color was still a recent innovation. "In our part of the world, people hardly dare to use color in their surroundings, and even less so at that time," says Panton von Halem. "Therefore, he consistently aimed to inspire people to embrace more color in their living spaces—and consequently, their lives."

As far back as 1958, Panton had utilized what would now be called color-drenching. His design for Kom-Igen Inn in Langesø Park, Denmark, had created a sensation—not just for the unveiling of his Cone chairs, but for the immersive use of red. "The main purpose of my work is to provoke people into using their imagination," Verner Panton said in a contemporary interview. "Most people spend their lives housed in dreary, gray-beige conformity, mortally afraid of using colors."

Panton's "total design" approach was again seen at his design of the Astoria Hotel in Trondheim, Norway in 1960. Cone and Heart Cone chairs, globe-shaped Topan lights and op-art Panton-designed Geometri Sheer textiles cocooned the rooms in dazzling reds and oranges.

But Panton's color-drenched interior concepts reached their apogee with the series of now-legendary Visiona exhibitions. Between 1968 and 1972, the German chemical company Bayer mounted an exhibition on an excursion boat during the Cologne Furniture Fair. Each year, a well-known designer would transform the boat into a technologically advanced essay on contemporary living. For Bayer, it was a way to promote new synthetic materials such as Dralon; for the designers, it was a platform for experimentation. "[Visiona] provided my father with a unique opportunity to realize his ideas free from functional requirements and market constraints," says Panton von Halem.

Panton took the helm for Visiona 0 in 1968 and Visiona II in 1970 (Panton coined the name 'Visiona' himself – until 1969, the exhibition was titled the 'Dralon Ship'). Visitors entered an immersive dream world of organic shapes and intense, enveloping colors. "While Visiona 0 could be described as a departure from traditional styles of living, Visiona II was entirely focused on the question of living in the world of tomorrow," says Vitra Design Museum. "It broke the traditional understanding of space with its clear ascription of functions, instead creating surroundings that were dedicated to well-being, communication, and relaxation." Panton von Halem adds: "As radical as these spaces may have seemed to most people, Panton did not regard the Visiona spaces as science fiction, but rather saw the spaces as an opportunity to challenge the conventional ideas of what a living space could look like."

"As radical as these spaces may have seemed to most people, Panton did not regard the Visiona spaces as science fiction, but rather saw the spaces as an opportunity to challenge the conventional ideas of what a living space could look like."

JOE COLOMBO

1969's Visiona I was created by Joe Colombo, an Italian industrial designer closely associated with Space-Age design. Colombo created several important pieces during the 1960s, including his Universale stacking chair for Kartell in 1965, and his Boby 3 Portable Storage System in 1969.

But it's his 1963 Eldra chair that has become one of the leading Space-Age classics. A futuristic throne of a chair in sculptural plastic with Dacron-covered polyurethane foam, it's a screen favorite: appearances include *Space 1999*, *The Hunger Games*, and Bond film *The Spy Who Loved Me*. "It oozes power," says AD100 interior designer Luis Laplace.

Colombo's Visiona I exhibition imagined the domestic set-up of a family of the future. It's a world of bountiful, sensuous leisure: ceiling-mounted televisions, swiveling walls, purple upholstery with integrated minibars, pod-like kitchens and bathrooms. The aesthetic is space-station of the future.

Many of Colombo's Visiona I innovations found their way into his 1972 Total Furnishing Unit—which has been exhibited at museums around the world including MoMA in New York and the Design Museum in London.

EARTHRISE

After a 22-month hiatus following the Apollo 1 disaster, crewed flights returned with the launch of Apollo 7 in October 1968. The crew spent 11 days in space and the mission included the first-ever live television broadcast from space. Just two months later, Apollo 8 set off to become the first crewed spacecraft to leave low-earth orbit and to fly around the moon.

The mission electrified the world. These were the first humans to escape Earth's gravity and to reach another celestial body. They were the first people to see the far side of the moon. And it was, at the time, the most-watched broadcast in the history of television. But the mission also gave us one of the most recognized images in history: *Earthrise*.

On Christmas Eve, 1968, Jim Lovell, Frank Borman, and Bill Anders were circling back around the moon when Anders, looking out of the window, saw an incredible sight.

NASA transcripts reveal the immediate effect it had on the astronauts. "Oh my God, look at that picture over there!" said Bill Anders. "There's the Earth coming up. Wow, is that pretty!"

Anders grabbed the camera and captured what would be an era-defining image. Until that moment, photographs of Earth had been from near-Earth orbit. Nothing like this had been seen before, and when the photograph was printed around the world, it brought with it a profound recalibration of our place in the universe. How alone our blue marble is in the endless void of space. And how fragile.

A few hours after Anders had taken the photo, his fellow crewman Lovell said: "The vast loneliness up here of the moon is awe-inspiring, and it makes you realize just what you have back there on Earth. The Earth from here is a grand oasis in the big vastness of space." On their return to Earth, the three astronauts were named 1968's *Time Magazine Men of the Year*.

APOLLO 11

There was now a real sense that a moon landing was within reach. But it was not inevitable that the Americans would take the prize. Apollo 8, after all, had not originally been scheduled for a moon flypast—it had been bounced into it by the CIA, who claimed (wrongly, as it happens) that the Soviets were planning their own manned lunar flypast. It wouldn't have been the first time the Soviets had pipped the U.S. to a major goal.

In fact, when Kennedy's moonshot speech had thrown down the gauntlet to the USSR, the Soviets had been careful not to pick it up. At first, they didn't take Kennedy's announcement seriously. Later, as Gemini began to show a sustained set of results, the Soviets refused to admit they were aiming for a moon landing; this would enable them to spike America's guns by claiming that the U.S. couldn't 'win' a goal the USSR had never been competing for. As Apollo 11's launch date neared, the Soviets held firm to this position. But U.S. intelligence and the international scientific community have always claimed otherwise.

THE LANDING

The iconography of the moon landing is seared into our folk memory. It's almost a foundational story of modern humanity. The soundbites (*The Eagle has landed; One small step*) and the images (the footprint on the regolith; the flag against a jet-black sky) have accrued the resonance of religious rites and mantras. But before re-treading that familiar ground, it's worth taking a look at some of the behind-the-scenes work that helped establish the Apollo mythology.

The sheer boldness, even chutzpah, of the moon landing as a grand geopolitical strategy is awe-inspiring. Apollo 11 was a generational opportunity to tell a world in flux that the democratic civilization posited a more dynamic, positive, and rewarding vision of the future than that offered by the Soviet Bloc. And the U.S. administration was leaving nothing to chance. In the months leading up to July 1969, legions of publicists, technicians, and strategists fanned out across the world, setting up television relay stations, regional news hubs, information resources, and image distribution centers. Film projectors and giant outside screens were put up in villages around India. Window displays were created in Berlin department stores. Embassy events were planned in Prague. Apollo souvenirs were shipped to Warsaw. Local journalists from across the world were brought to Houston to train, meet the astronauts, and explore NASA's facilities so that they could return to their respective countries as Apollo experts.

Venues and transport were booked for a 38-day world tour that would follow the moon landing, taking the astronauts to countries across South America, Asia, and Europe. Strategically chosen cities included Tehran, Ankara, Belgrade, Kinshasa, Mumbai, and Tokyo. It was the PR event of the century.

None of this takes away from the incredible achievement itself. On the contrary, the messaging is a reflection of the extraordinary level of confidence and planning that enabled the Americans to execute the moon landing. But it also demonstrates how space was threaded through the culture of the time, never far from the news, deeply entwined with the fabric of life, from politics and the Cold War to design, art, fashion, music, interiors, and architecture.

THE EAGLE HAS LANDED

The weather in Florida was cloudy on the morning of 16 July 1969, with thunderstorms threatening to break cover. But by lunchtime, the clouds thinned out; the astronauts' day of destiny would not be delayed, and the Saturn V rocket blasted Apollo 11 into space to begin its three-day journey to the moon.

On 20 July, schoolchildren and office workers around the world were given the day off, and they began to gather around any television screen they could find. Neil Armstrong and Buzz Aldrin, by now in orbit around the moon, parted ways with Michael Collins, who for the next few days would be the loneliest man alive as he awaited their return on the command module. Armstrong and Aldrin climbed into the Eagle lunar module and descended to the surface of the moon, touching down 12 minutes later in the Sea of Tranquility.

PEAK SPACE-AGE DESIGN

We know now that what looked like the start of things was in reality the end of things. Project Apollo had achieved its goal. Soon, we'd leave the moon and not return.

But in the euphoria of the moon landings, things could not have looked more different. It was the high point of the Space Age; space was the hottest topic and global mainstream interest injected a massive shot of energy into Space-Age design and influence. It was seen everywhere, from David Bowie's *Space Oddity*—released a month after the landing—to JVC's space-helmeted Videosphere television.

The Apollo period also heralded a maturation of Space-Age designers, with some of their greatest accomplishments: Verner Panton's VP Globe pendant lamp, the Vitra Gravitino 541, and the Camaleonda Sofa by Mario Bellini—all three of which are still highly desirable and still in production today.

And at a time when it seemed reasonable to assume that we'd be living in space within a few decades, designers began to consider how that might look.

Sofa design is a classic example. Modular sofas had been around since the 1940s, but now they became sprawling and heroic, made for fabulous, futuristic lifestyles. Rigid forms were out; enveloping, sensual, organic shapes were in. These were statement sofas that could belong in a Lake Como villa or on a space station orbiting the moon. Sitting upright was declasse; sofas were for slumbering, socializing, or partying.

The pieces created at this pinnacle of creativity are still among the most desirable now. Go to Miami's Design District today and you'll find the Togo dominating Ligne Roset's flagship store on one side of the street and the Camaleonda dominating the B&B Italia store on the other.

Mario Bellini designed the Camaleonda in 1970; the name is a portmanteau of the Italian words for chameleon and wave. It was unveiled by B&B Italia in 1972 and it was a hit, appearing—alongside Joe Colombo's Total Furnishing Unit—in MoMA's *Italy: The New Domestic Landscape* exhibition. With its marshmallow-like appearance, the Camaleonda blended 70s Italian flair with a futuristic space-aesthetic; and it fits into that category of Instagrammable design that makes it as popular now as it was in the 1970s.

Of equal stature is the iconic Togo, designed by Michel Ducaroy for Ligne Roset. Unveiled at Paris's Salon des Arts Ménagers in 1973, its crushed, slouchy appearance and lack of a base initially surprised, then won over the public. And not unlike the Camaleonda, it's become a super-hot item in the last few years and a mainstay of high-end interior design projects.

Two of the most exuberant examples from the era come from Swiss company De Sede. The 1972 DS-600 Snake—so modular that it was awarded the world's longest sofa by the *Guinness Book of Records*—is formed in such a way that it can snake through vast rooms, the individual seats facing in either direction. It is perhaps the ultimate statement sofa—equally at home in a loft apartment or the Palace of Versailles. Also made by De Sede is the 1974 DS-1025 Terrazza, which resembles an upholstered terraced rice paddy. Favored by today's leading interior designers such as Kelly Wearstler and Martyn Lawrence Bullard, its 70s glam credentials were not harmed by appearances in a Mick Jagger photoshoot and the cult sci-fi film *Logan's Run*. Interior designer Adam Charlap Hyman, speaking in *Architectural Digest*, says: "They have this cheeky, orgy vibe and encourage all these weird ways of sitting. It's like something from outer space landed in your living room."

Pierre Paulin took a different approach, creating a series of exceptional modular pieces that experimented with the very essence and nature of furniture. "Between 1968 and 1972, my father was thinking that the future of furniture was for it to disappear," says his son Benjamin Paulin. "So, then it becomes about the articulation of the floors."

Dune, Tapis-Siège, and Déclive are prototypes that were designed between 1968 and 1972, but are only now being produced, in limited edition, by Paulin Paulin Paulin. And they really do challenge the boundary between furniture and room. Dune is almost a room in itself, with integrated tables that can be fixed at any intersection between the modules. Current owners include Frank Ocean and Kanye West.

"Modular sofas had been around since the 1940s, but now they became sprawling and heroic, made for fabulous, futuristic lifestyles"

AFTER THE EAGLE

The dream that began with Kennedy's audacious plan to reach the moon had reached its fulfillment. The landing had electrified the world and exerted an influence on culture that would last for generations.

Space exploration between 1969 and 1972 continued. The Soviets launched the first-ever space station, the Salyut 1, and David Scott, commander of the Apollo 15 mission, became the first person to drive on the moon. The Soviet Union completed the first soft landing on Mars; shortly after, Pioneer 10 became the first probe to enter the asteroid belt and leave the inner Solar System.

But strangely, while design and culture would remain space-obsessed for many more years, interest in the Apollo program itself tailed off rapidly. "After the first lunar landing, the space race lost a lot of the tension that was driving it in the early 1960s," says Teasel Muir-Harmony. "For most people, the space race was relatively done."

By Apollo 13 in April 1970, less than a year after the moon landing, the media barely bothered turning up. It's only when an oxygen tank ruptured and the mission turned into a near-disaster that the TV cameras hot-footed it back to Mission Control, reporting to a public now riveted because three astronauts, in a dysfunctional craft several hundred thousand miles away from Earth would likely die. "The fact that they didn't is one of the remarkable success stories in NASA history," says Roger D. Launius.

The final Apollo crewed mission took place in December 1972. By now, the Watergate Scandal had broken, and public life in America through the Apollo years had perhaps made a journey from earnestness to cynicism. When the boot of Mission Commander Eugene Cernan stepped off the lunar surface and back into the lunar module, no one knew it was the last time anyone would set foot on the moon for what is now over half a century and counting. But at the time, no one paid much attention. Apollo, which began with tragedy and soared to such triumph, had ended with indifference.

Apollo 11 Lunar Module during separation from the Command Module prior to its descent to the lunar surface, July 1969

Apollo 11 astronaut Buzz Aldrin takes his first step onto the surface of the Moon, July 1969

Apollo 11 astronaut Buzz Aldrin walks on the surface of the moon, July 1969

Buzz Aldrin beside the lunar module, July 1969

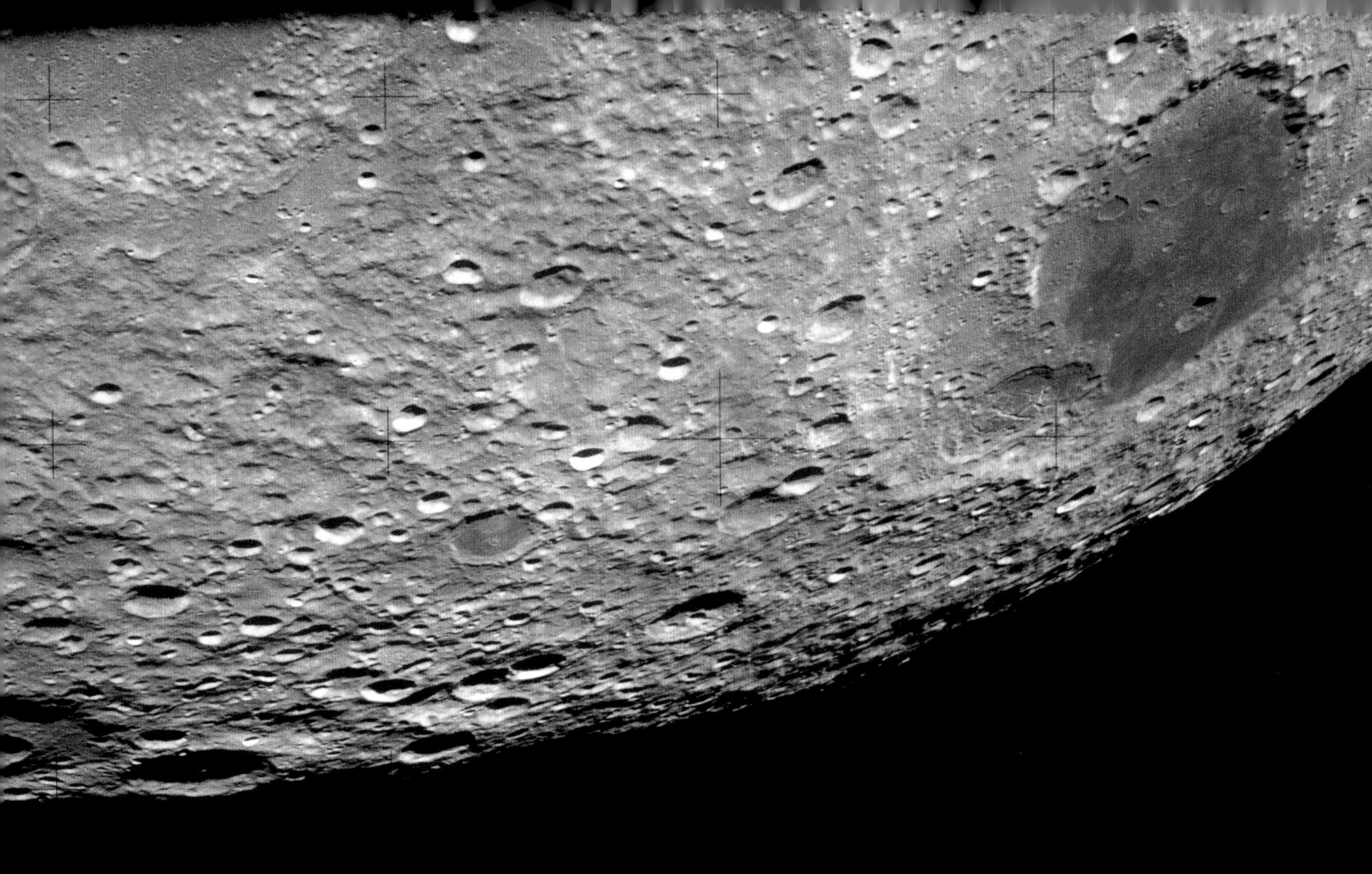

Oblique view of lunar far-side, photographed from Apollo 13 spacecraft, 1970.

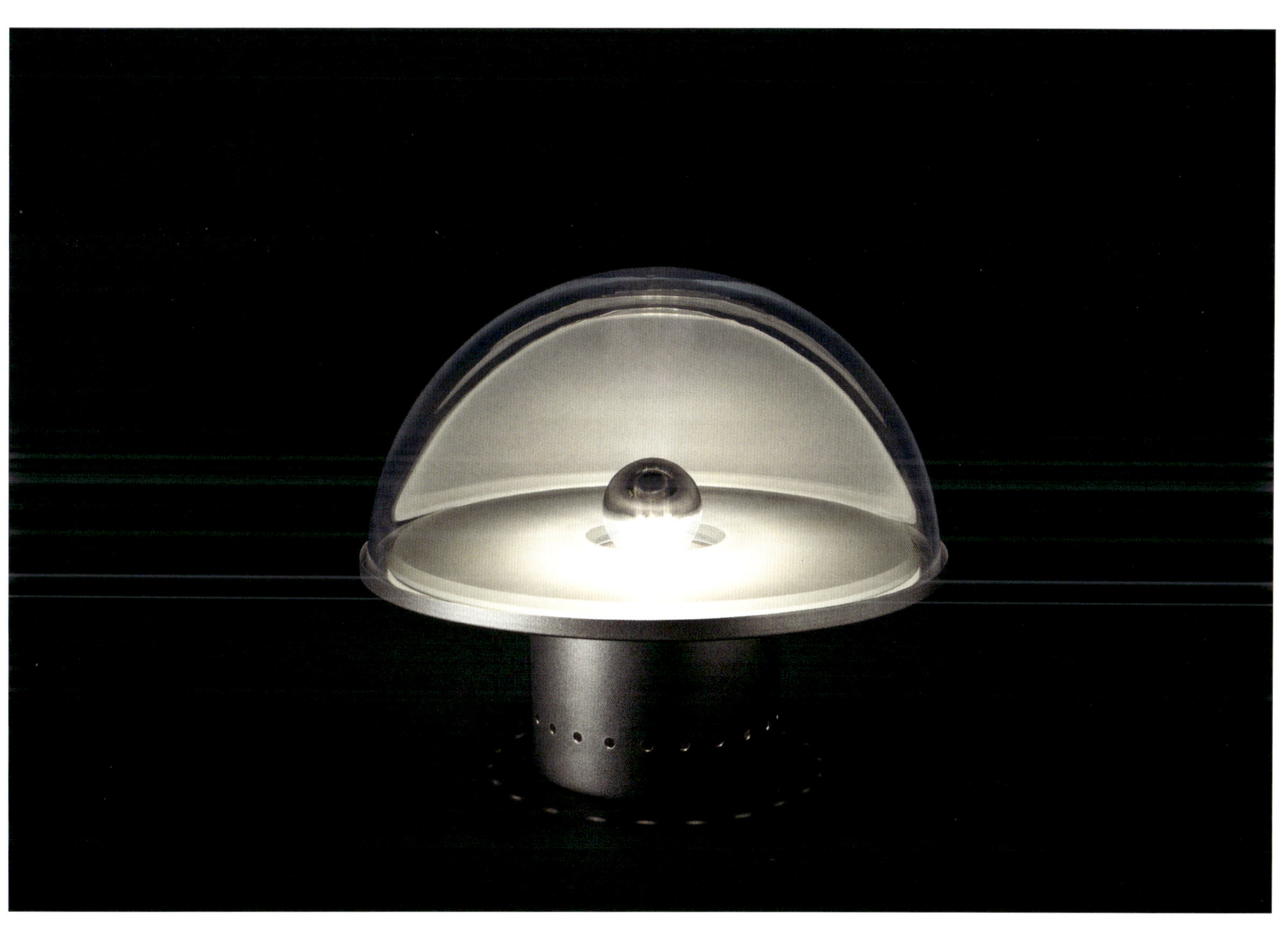

Siderea by Alberto Rosselli, courtesy of TATO, 1969

Astronaut Fred W. Haise Jr. practices operation of the 16-millimeter motion picture camera to be used during the Apollo 13 mission, 1970

JVC Videosphere Television, 1970

View of the Earth seen by the Apollo 17 crew traveling toward the moon, December 1972

VP Globe pendant photographed by Joe Kramm, designed by Verner Panton in 1969

Maurice-Claude Vidili's Sphère d'isolement S2, 1971

HERE MEN FROM THE PLANET EARTH
FIRST SET FOOT UPON THE MOON
JULY 1969, A. D.

WE CAME IN PEACE FOR ALL MANKIND

NEIL A. ARMSTRONG
ASTRONAUT

MICHAEL COLLINS
ASTRONAUT

EDWIN E. ALDRIN, JR.
ASTRONAUT

RICHARD NIXON
PRESIDENT, UNITED STATES OF AMERICA

Apollo 11 stainless steel lunar plaque, attached to the descent stage of the Lunar Module to be left permanently on the lunar surface, 1969

B&B Italia Serie Up, designed by Gaetano Pesce, promotional archive images, 1969

B&B Italia Serie Up, designed by Gaetano Pesce, promotional archive image, 1969

Knut Hesterberg Lounge Chair, 1971 (courtesy Mass Modern Design)

Pierre Paulin Décliven°3, 1970

Pierre Paulin Dune, 1970

Lemon Sole Lounge Chairs by Kwok Hoï Chan for Steiner, 1971 (courtesy Mass Modern Design)

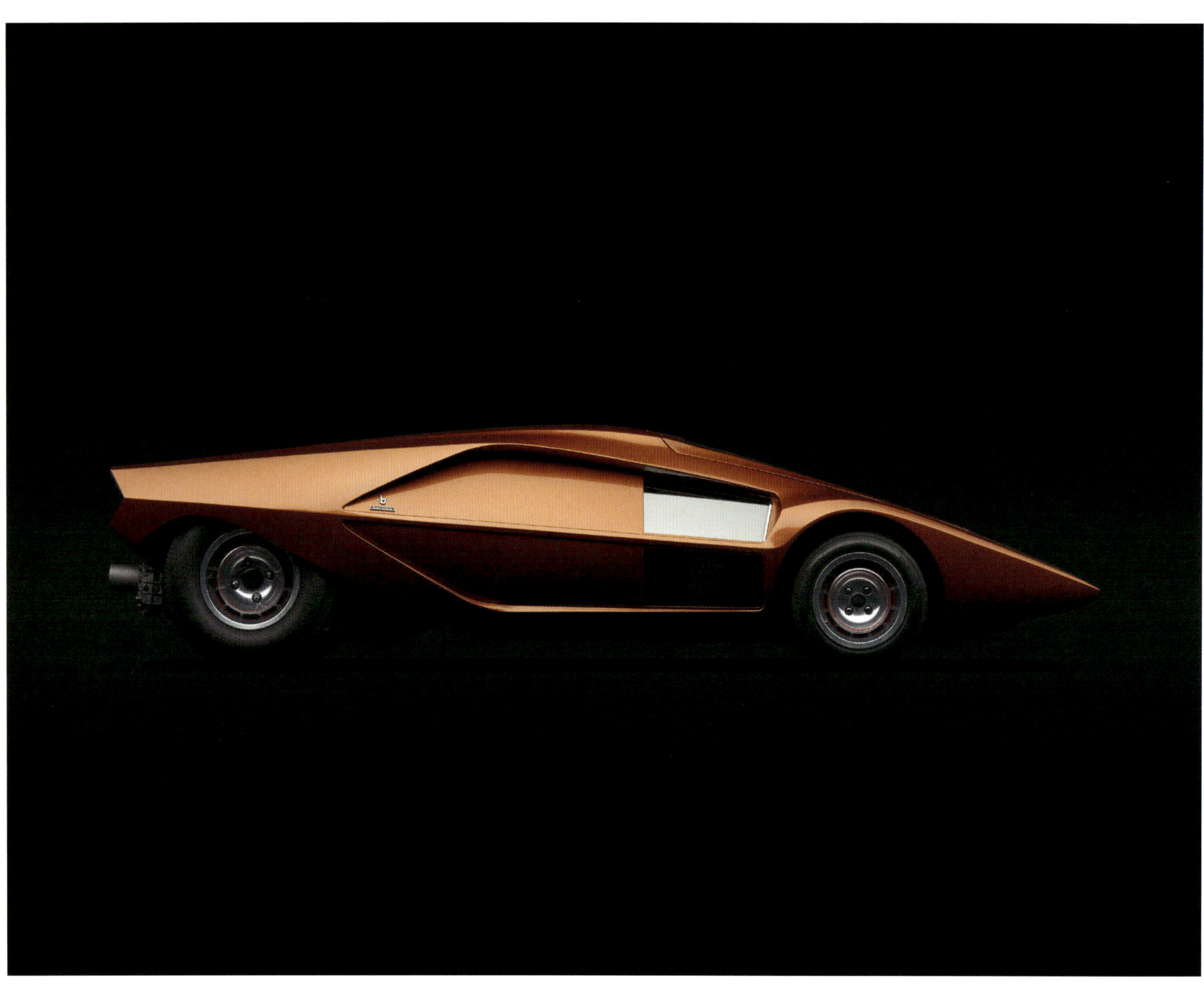

Lancia Stratos Zero, 1970

Soriana Lounge Chairs by Tobia and Afra Scarpa for Cassina, 1971 (courtesy Modest Furniture)

Apollo 11 Lunar Module on the lunar surface, 1969

Astronaut Buzz Aldrin, pilot of the first lunar landing mission, beside the deployed United States flag, 1969

Ticker-tape parade for the Apollo 11 astronauts, 1969

Pistillo Lamp by Studio Tetrarch for Valenti Luce, 1969 (Modest Furniture)

Apollo 12 astronaut Alan Bean holding a lunar soil sample container, November 1969

Apollo 9 Command Module, March 1969

Apollo 9 Lunar Module, March 1969

The World Clock, East Berlin, East Germany, 1969

Luigi Colani Sadima lounge chair by BASF Germany, 1970 (courtesy Mass Modern Design)

Verpan Cloverleaf Sofa, design by Verner Panton / © Verner Panton Design AG & Verpan A/S 1969

B&B Italia Camaleonda by Mario Bellini, 1971

Apollo 14 Command Module approaches touchdown in the South Pacific, February 1971

Olivier Mourgue interior for the Visiona 3 exhibition, 1972

B&B Italia Camaleonda by Mario Bellini, 1970

Prisma sofa and armchair by Augusto Betti, archive Habitat Sintoni catalog, 1971

Prisma sofa and armchair by Augusto Betti, Paradisoterrestre, designed in 1971

B&B Italia Serie Up: vacuum packages, 1969

Apollo 16 crew training, January 1972

(previous pages and above) Verner Panton landscaped interior for the Visiona II exhibition in 1968.
Design by Verner Panton, www.verner-panton.com © Verner Panton

Apollo exhibition at the U.S. pavilion at Expo 70—the World Fair in Osaka, Japan, 1970

Apollo exhibition at the U.S. pavilion at Expo 70—the World Fair in Osaka, Japan, 1970

Apollo 17 commander Eugene A. Cernan approaches the parked Lunar Roving Vehicle with South Massif in the background, December 1972

Chairs by Luigi Colani at Morentz, 1970s

Joe Colombo installation for Bayer's Visiona I exhibition, 1969 in Cologne, Germany

Maurice Calka desk, 1969

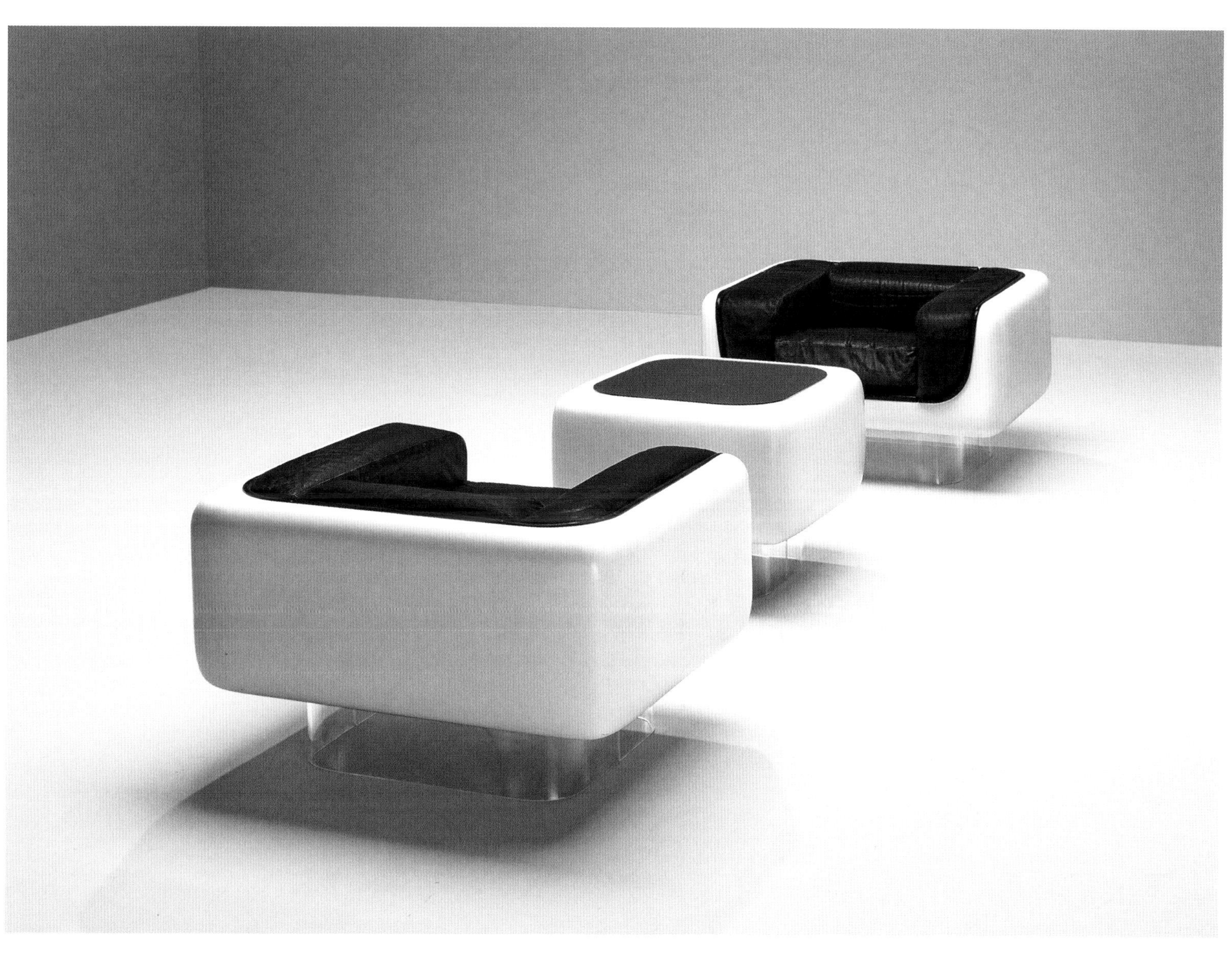

William Andrus for Steelcase living room set in fiberglass and leather at Morentz, 1972

Apollo 16 Command/Service Module, April 1972

Boris Tabacoff Lounge Chair, 1971 (City Furniture)

Apollo 17 astronaut Harrison Schmitt next to U.S. flag with Earth in the background, December 1972

Zeus Table Lamp by Cini Boeri for Gavina, 1971 (courtesy Modest Furniture)

Apollo 14 astronaut Edgar D. Mitchell with a TV camera, February 1971

Pierre Paulin Élysée Chair, 1971

Apollo 17 astronaut Harrison Schmitt next to Tracy's Rock lunar boulder during the final-ever spacewalk, photographed by Eugene Cernan, the last person to walk on the moon, December 1972

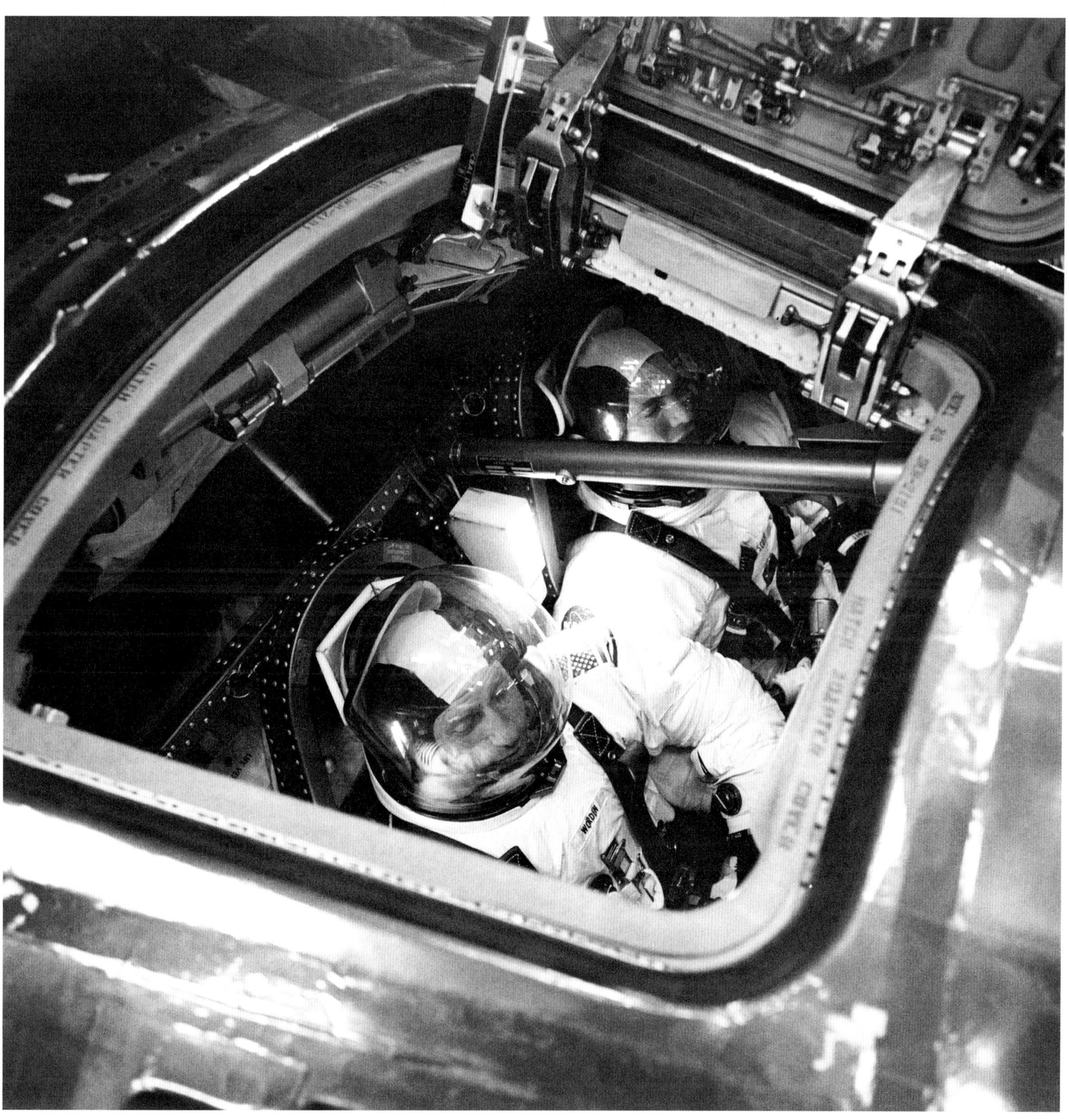

Crew members inside the Apollo 15 Command Module during simulation training at the Kennedy Space Center, March 1971

Nikolaos Xasteros Micro-House, France, 1969

View of Earth rising above the lunar horizon over the Ritz Crater taken during the Apollo 17 mission, December 1972

Prinz Sound Stereo, 1970

Apollo 17 during launch countdown, December 1972

Apollo 11 Saturn V rocket leaves the Vehicle Assembly Building on the journey to the launch pad, May 1969

SPACE STATION 1973–1986

PART IV

The 1950s had put satellites in space. The 60s had put humans on the moon. But the messy, complicated decade that followed saw a more fractured and exhausted world with less appetite for competitive adventures in space. The great tensions that drove the space race had dissipated as soon as Apollo 11's astronauts had fulfilled Kennedy's great challenge by arriving safely back from the moon. By 1973, the Nixon administration was mired in Vietnam, the Watergate scandal, and the Oil Shock, when global oil prices tripled. While the latter didn't hurt the Soviets, with their vast natural resources, they had run their space program since the 1950s on a relative shoestring. Now under Leonid Brezhnev, the 70s were a dismal decade for the Soviet economy, and space spending wasn't likely to ramp up any time soon.

Yet while nothing matched the moon landing as a mass shared experience (and probably wouldn't until 9/11, for very different reasons), space progress continued at pace. "The 1970s are often seen as the doldrums in space history," says William P. Barry, "but a lot of important things happened then, especially the development of the first space stations, the fitful start of cooperation of the U.S. and USSR in space, the development of the Space Shuttle (though it wouldn't fly until the 1980s) and a huge leap forward in robotic planetary and space science exploration."

And space remained a major cultural driver throughout the decade and into the next, from Bond films to videogames and high-end Italian design.

"Space remained a major cultural driver throughout the decade and into the next, from Bond films to videogames and high-end Italian design."

SPACE-AGE ARCHITECTURE IN THE SOVIET BLOC

Space remained a major influence on Eastern Bloc architecture, too. Dotted throughout the former Soviet sphere, from Russia to Bosnia and Herzegovina, is a legacy of eerie, evocative monuments to the Soviet space era. The USSR was, to its end in 1991, justifiably proud of its space program. It also remained a major propaganda tool throughout its empire: the use of technological prowess to tame the vast chaos of the cosmos was a potent metaphor for the use of scientific socialism to tame the vagaries of human avarice. Architectural celebrations of space exploration acted as this metaphor's avatars throughout the Warsaw Pact realm.

Perhaps the first of these was the 1964 Monument to the Conquerors of Space in Moscow. Conceived in 1958 and completed in 1964, it exactly tracks the period of Soviet primacy in the space race. Designed by sculptor Andrey Faydysh-Krandievsky, it's a monumental, towering sculpture of a rocket thrusting toward space—a highly visible symbol of Soviet space power. It's breathtaking in ambition and there's something of the boldness of Eero Saarinen's Gateway Arch about it.

But more haunting are the monuments that came after, in the far reaches of the Soviet Union's satellites. Perched high on the remote peaks of the Balkan Mountains is a colossal concrete flying saucer—the ruins of the 1981 Buzludzha Monument in Bulgaria, built between 1974 and 1981 to commemorate the founding of the Bulgarian Socialist Party.

Thousands of miles to the east is the 1970 Memorial for the 50th Anniversary of Soviet Armenia, a soaring, Modernist, Space-Age construction that towers above the city of Dilijan like an alien spacecraft. There's the Brutalist, rocket-shaped Monument to Fallen Fighters at Bratunac in Republic Srpska, Bosnia and Herzegovina from 1978. And the 1971 "Flying Saucer" building in Kyiv by Ukranian architect Florian Yuriev.

What gives this branch of Space-Age architectural design its deeply affecting and melancholic power is that these monuments and buildings are celebrations of a future that never arrived, created by a vanished civilization. Vincent Fournier, who has captured many of these monuments in his work *Kosmic Memories*, says: "If all these buildings have different functions, commemorative, political, institutional, their forms testify to the same breath: the invention of a future imbued with science fiction. Brutalist, futuristic, utopian, mystical, esoteric beauty... these sentinels embody the dream of a future that is always to come."

PALAIS BULLES

Space did not just inspire Warsaw Pact architecture in the 1970s and 80s. Palais Bulles, on the French Riviera, is a sprawling, fantastical collection of organic pods and spheres overlooking the Mediterranean. Designed by Hungarian architect Antti Lovag for French industrialist Pierre Bernard, it was later bought by Pierre Cardin—one of the fathers of Space-Age fashion. Cardin continued to develop it with Lovag, turning it into what he described as "my bit of paradise." Designed in the 1970s and completed in the 80s, it nevertheless transmits a 1960s vision of the Space Age. And where the Warsaw Pact Space-Age architecture is austerely utopian, Palais Bulles is decadently so—more Roger Vadim's *Barbarella* than Andrei Tarkovsky's *Solaris*.

ITALIAN LIGHTING DESIGN

Space-Age aesthetics had a major impact on Italian lighting designers throughout the mid-century era, from Stilnovo—who had pioneered the Sputnik chandelier—to Gio Ponti and Angelo Gaetano Sciolari. This continued well into the 1970s: In 1972, Harvey Guzzini designed the Sorella lamp, a sculptural table light created from acrylic with an internal iron counterweight. It had an elegantly futuristic quality and became a Space-Age screen icon, appearing extensively in the 1970s British TV series *Space 1999* (at the time, the most expensive series produced for British TV) and the 1979 James Bond film *Moonraker*.

Another 1970s icon—which appears continually in contemporary residential and hotel interior design projects—is the Atollo lamp, designed in 1977 for Oluce by Vico Magistretti. Minimal, geometric, and elegant, it is described by Architonic as telling "the story of a rocket on its way to a spherical body, possibly the moon or a more distant planet." The base is almost identical in proportions to the Apollo Command Module.

"Where the Warsaw Pact Space-Age architecture is austerely utopian, Palais Bulles is decadently so."

AUDIO-VISUAL PRODUCT DESIGN

Product design, too, was heavily space-influenced in the 1970s and early 80s. The JVC Videosphere was a space helmet-shaped television, usually in white or orange, in production from its first iteration in 1970 until the 1980s. Now to be found in design museums throughout the world, it's probably one of the most recognizable pieces of Space-Age-influenced design globally. Of a similar ilk is the early 1970s PrinzSound Stereo "Spaceball" radio and 8-track player, manufactured by Weltron. But at the apex of Space-Age audio-visual design icons are two Stereo Commanders: the 1968 C-105 Hi-Fi Console by Italian photographer and designer Willy Rizzo, and the 1974 Stereo Commander Luxus, designed by Theo Schmitz for Rosita.

APOLLO-SOYUZ AND A HANDSHAKE IN SPACE

An event happened in the middle of the 1970s which some read as heralding the end of the space race (there's no universal agreement on when the space race drew to a close—for some, it was the moment the Eagle had touched down; for others, the mid-1980s).

But in 1975, an American Apollo spacecraft docked with a Soviet Soyuz capsule 140 miles (230km) above the Earth. Millions watched as astronaut Thomas P. Stafford and cosmonaut Alexei Leonard reached through the dock and grasped each others' hands. The handshake marked a historic moment of détente between the superpowers.

What did it mean? It demonstrated that the Soviet Union and the U.S. could come together as partners. It freed each country from defining its space program against the other. And it was a potent symbol of détente.

But it didn't lead to a great deal in terms of space cooperation, or to closer relations between the superpowers. And it didn't stop the Soviets invading Afghanistan in 1979.

In a strange sort of way, the 1970s marked a return to Wernher von Braun and NASA's 1959 long-term plan which had been derailed by Kennedy's decade-long detour to the moon. Von Braun had always imagined a reusable winged spacecraft that would service a space station. In Skylab, they had a space station. And now they began planning the Space Shuttle—a winged reusable spacecraft.

Nixon approved the Space Shuttle in 1972. Construction began in 1975 and testing on the finished orbiter began in 1979—the year Roger Moore starred in *Moonraker*, a Bond film which involved a hijacked Space Shuttle with a showdown on Drax's space station. That the once-hardened secret agent now found himself in a space romp is a testament both to the domination of space in the 1970s and to the colossal success of 1977's *Star Wars*.

Star Wars was, in fact, the highest-grossing movie of the 1970s. And *Space Invaders* was the highest-grossing videogame of the 1970s. Across the world, the Apollo 13 splashdown was the most-watched TV event of the 1970s. In other words, by the time the first Space Shuttle took off in 1981, space was a huge deal in the public imagination, influencing cinema, architecture, fashion, furniture design, product design, and music—from the natural affinity between glam disco and Space-Age fashion, to the Asha Puthli-influenced future electro-disco of Giorgio Moroder and Donna Summer—and on to the jagged, crystalline synths and attitude of 70s and 80s New Wave.

THE SPACE AGE DESIGN MOVEMENT

From the 1950s through to the 1980s, space exploration exerted an extraordinary influence on mainstream culture, underground culture, and all manner of subcultures.

But the Space Age Design Movement—to collectively group together the disparate creatives who drank from the same well and shared a unique era—was about more than just a nod to the aesthetics of a real or imagined Space Age. It was about innovation, expanding horizons, and optimism—a belief that the future was a wonderful place and a hunger to draw it closer.

This optimism had been inspired, not deterred, by the Apollo 1 tragedy, the Apollo 13 near-tragedy, and the Soyuz 1 tragedy. But there was something different about what happened on 28 January 1986, which is why it marks the end of this movement that had begun with Sputnik 29 years before.

Everyone at school in the 1980s remembers the Challenger Space Shuttle disaster. From the beginning, it was not a normal flight, so had received more media attention than usual. The mission itself was not atypical: to deploy a communications satellite and study Halley's Comet. But this time, the crew included a non-astronaut, Christina McAuliffe, a schoolteacher from New Hampshire who had joined as part of Ronald Reagan's *Teacher In Space* program. The idea was that McAuliffe's presence in space would inspire young people to engage with science. She'd also be teaching a lesson from the Shuttle while in space.

Around the world, school children watched live as Challenger lifted off into a clear blue sky from Cape Canaveral at 11:38 am. The cameras tracked the shuttle as it thrust into the upper atmosphere, strapped to the enormous booster rocket. Moments later, it was gone, replaced with a vast vapor trail that spread like eviscerated entrails across the dome of the sky. The freezing weather that morning had led a rubber seal to fail in the right-hand rocket booster, with calamitous results.

Ronald Reagan canceled his State of the Union address that night; instead, he delivered a eulogy to the shocked American nation: "We've never had a tragedy like this. And perhaps we've forgotten the courage it took for the crew of the shuttle."

Later in the address, he says: "We've grown used to wonders in this century. It's hard to dazzle us. But for 25 years the United States space program has been doing just that. We've grown used to the idea of space, and perhaps we forget that we've only just begun. We're still pioneers. They, the members of the Challenger crew, were pioneers."

The Challenger Disaster marks the end of that period when space exploration was still fresh, still new, and still freighted with the pioneering dreams of a generation that had survived the war and set out to build a new future. By 1986, the American Dream had taken on a less cohesive, less fraternal, more individualized character.

The Soviet Dream was all but over—within six years, the Soviet Union would collapse.

The designers of the 1950s, 60s and 70s, with all the energy, new ideas, and idealism of youth, were growing old, their ground-breaking new materials now commonplace or even problematic. With the 1980s now immersed in their own aesthetic flavors, the 1970s looked gauche, the 60s kitsch, and the 50s remote. It was the end of an era.

"From the 1950s through to the 1980s, space exploration exerted an extraordinary influence on mainstream culture, underground culture, and all manner of subcultures."

Armenia, Kosmic Memories, 2022. Courtesy of the artist Vincent Fournier. Work depicts the Monument to the 50th Anniversary of Soviet Armenia, 1970

The Soviet Union’s Soyuz 19 spacecraft during the Apollo-Soyuz Test Project, July 1975

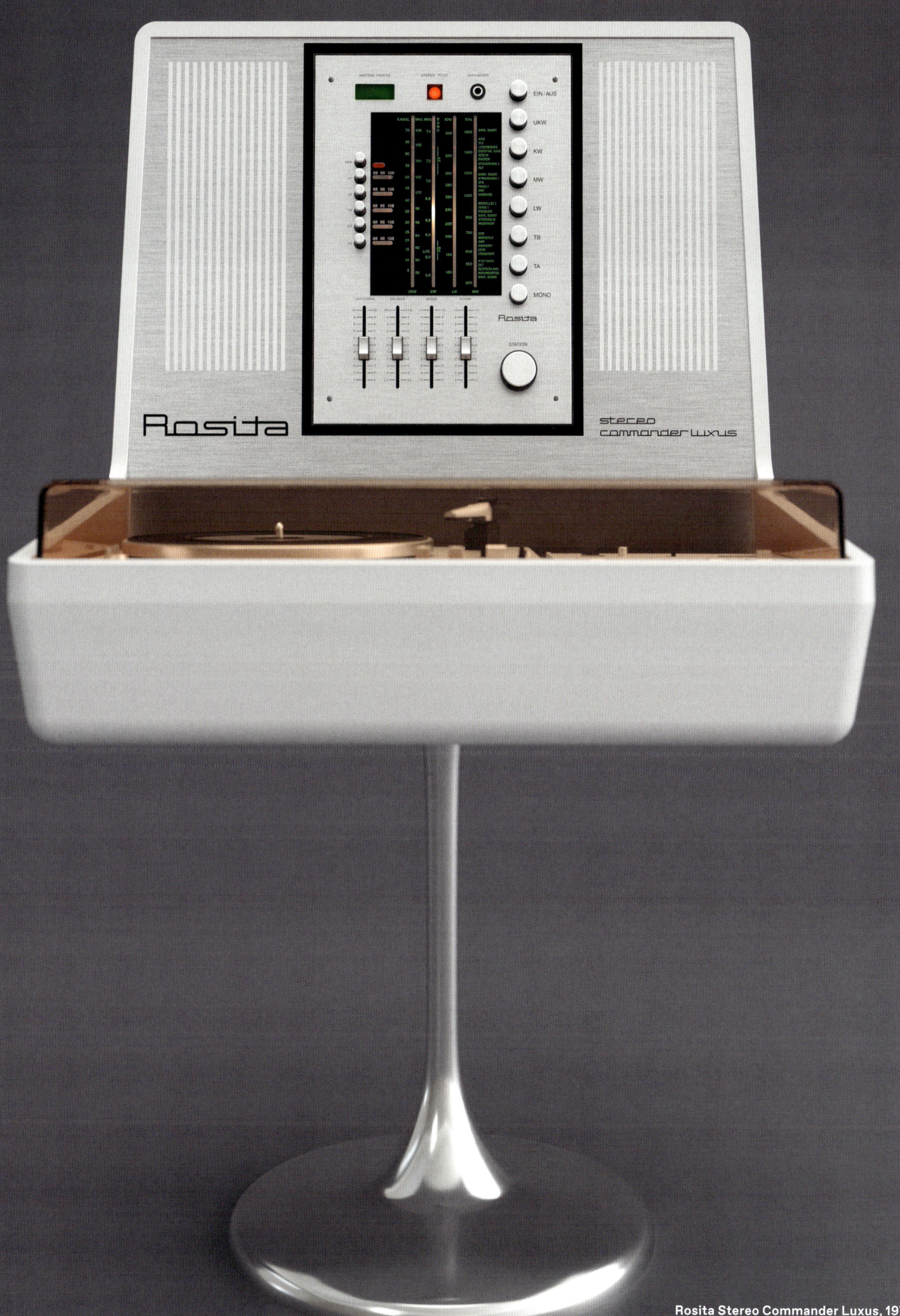

Rosita Stereo Commander Luxus, 1974,
rendered by Jason Wray

The Apollo 14 Command and Service Modules (above), photographed from the Lunar Module in 1971, were an influence on the Atollo (right), designed by Vico Magistretti for Oluce in 1977

Astronaut Bruce McCandless II performs the first-ever untethered spacewalk during a Challenger Space Shuttle mission, February 1984

DS-1025 gold-edition sofa by De Sede, 1974

DS-1025 sofa by De Sede, 1974

Soviet Soyuz spacecraft on display at the 30th International Aeronautics and Space Exhibition in Paris, 1973

Archive promotional image of the 1973 Ligne Roset Togo modular sofa designed by Michel Ducaroy

WES
MONTGOMERY
MEMORIAL
Toys by Artists

Space Shuttle development: testing a 0.36 scale model in February 1976

Smoke Plia Chairs by Giancarlo Piretti for Anonima Castelli, 1970s (courtesy Kooloo Modern)

Palais Bulles, French Riviera, designed 1970s

Official emblem for NASA's Skylab Program, 1973

Ligne Roset Togo modular sofa designed by Michel Ducaroy in 1973

Buzludzha#1, Kosmic Memories, 2020. Courtesy of the artist Vincent Fournier.
Work depicts the Monument House of the Bulgarian Communist Party (Buzludzha Monument), inaugurated in 1981

Skylab Space Station, February 1974

Verner Panton System 1-2-3 Dining Chair, 1973 Design by Verner Panton / © Verner Panton Design AG & Verpan A/S

LEGACY

PART V

“Most importantly, we found ourselves.”

William P. Barry, former chief historian, NASA

Following the 1980s, it’s fair to say that space was not on the cultural agenda for 30 years at least. There were moments, of course; Air’s 1998 album *Moon Safari* channeled a louche, dreamy, Space-Aged 1960s vibe; it was the audio love-child of Pierre Paulin and Verner Panton, and it changed the temperature of music for several years. And there were films, *Gravity* and *Interstellar* among them. A subsection of people would always remain interested in space, but the point is that space didn’t enter the zeitgeist, and that’s because it didn’t speak to the needs and preoccupations of people living in the 1990s, who were more concerned with the end of the Cold War and a relatively benign, newly globalized world order; or in the 2000s, with all the agonies of the Global War on Terror; or the post-financial-crash 2010s and so on. Space was divorced from the currents moving beneath society, whereas in the 1950s, the space race had exploded out of those very currents—with space exploration becoming a lightning rod for the aspirations of those alive at the time.

We now find ourselves at the cusp of a new space race—this time between Asian neighbors jostling for prestige. A generation of tech billionaires brought up on *Star Trek* are creating a thriving private space sector. NASA is now focused on Artemis and an imminent return to the moon. The increasing tempo of all this activity has cut through and is leading to a renewal of interest in the events of the Space Age era. The past few years have seen a rapid and dramatic reappraisal of the place space holds in our culture. Across many spheres, space is back on the agenda and back in fashion.

Europe’s largest infrastructure project of recent years—London’s Elizabeth Line—is full of Space-Age influence. Spanish studio Masquespacio has created a restaurant in Milan modeled on a space station. Space-Age design, lumped together for years with the general canon of mid-century work, is now being reappraised in its own right. Landmark interior design projects in New York, L.A., and London are consistently seasoned with Camaleonda sofas, Joe Colombo chairs, and Sputnik chandeliers. European gallerists, in particular, have been quick to notice the magnetic pull of Space-Age design as a cohesive movement, readier to label vintage design pieces as belonging to the Space-Age canon, and more vocal advocates for it. Emerging superstar designers such as Giampiero Tagliaferri quote Space-Age design as a cornerstone of their aesthetic. French visual artists such as Vincent Fournier put the Space Age at the core of their work.

And a new, 21st-century Space Age Design Movement is gathering pace. Some of the most vibrant design and interior design is coming from India and China right now. Chinese designers in particular are creating projects of staggering complexity and scale; and a majority of those who are breaking through internationally are creating Space-Age work in a way not seen in the world since the 1970s. There’s nothing nostalgic about their work; they are taking the principles of the Space Age Design Movement—optimism, new materials, an exploration of lifestyle, and space influence—and applying them to the contemporary design landscape. Like European and American designers during the space race years, Chinese designers today have a powerful sense of optimism, even destiny, about the future and a lack of aesthetic baggage about the past. Mid-century designers Eero Saarinen and Verner Panton would likely feel great kinship with contemporary designers such as Peng Zheng and Eason Zhu.

To appraise the mid-century Space Age Design Movement is to recognize how its creative impetus and leading designers have come of age as a significantly influential force across contemporary design. But it’s also to appreciate the gravitational pull of nostalgia for the era—which accounts for the phenomenal increase in value of Space Age design and space race memorabilia. In a strange echo from the past, a *New York Times* headline from this year proclaims: *U.S. Fears Russia Might Put a Nuclear Weapon in Space*. An OpEd in the same paper asks: *Is This a Sputnik Moment?*

It demonstrates how impactful that era remains to us, as if our collective consciousness still carries the hopes of its endeavors and the scars of its traumas. It is the reason why the design icons of the Space Age continue to hold such mesmeric juju. They are inherently sculptural and beautiful, but they are also emissaries from a shinier and more optimistic world.

Let’s give the last word to William P. Barry, who was for many years NASA’s chief historian. His take on the lasting impact of the space race era is multifold; he believes, for example, that our smartphones wouldn’t exist without the rapid computing advancements made possible by Apollo. But he ends like this:

“Most importantly, we found ourselves. Those pictures of our beautiful, fragile planet that came out of the space race had a galvanizing effect on many aspects of our lives. The ripple effects of understanding that our Earth is unique in being hospitable for human life and that we are all in this together continue to be a source of hope for the future.”

The ongoing influence of the space age is seen everywhere, with the seminal images of the era such as Stanley Kubrick's *2001: A Space Odyssey* (below left) reflected in the work of contemporary Chinese architect and designer Wenqiang Li of PIG Design (right, as featured in the Andrew Martin International Interior Design Review Volume 26) and (above left) London's 2022 Elizabeth Line stations.

Space-age influences are again seen on continents around the world. Space-age lighting arrays can be seen in London's contemporary Elizabeth Line Station at Paddington (bottom right), Eero Saarinen's 1962 TWA Flight Center in New York (top right), now restored as the TWA Hotel, and the ATLATL restaurant in Shanghai (above) by Chinese design firm Various Associates, 2020.

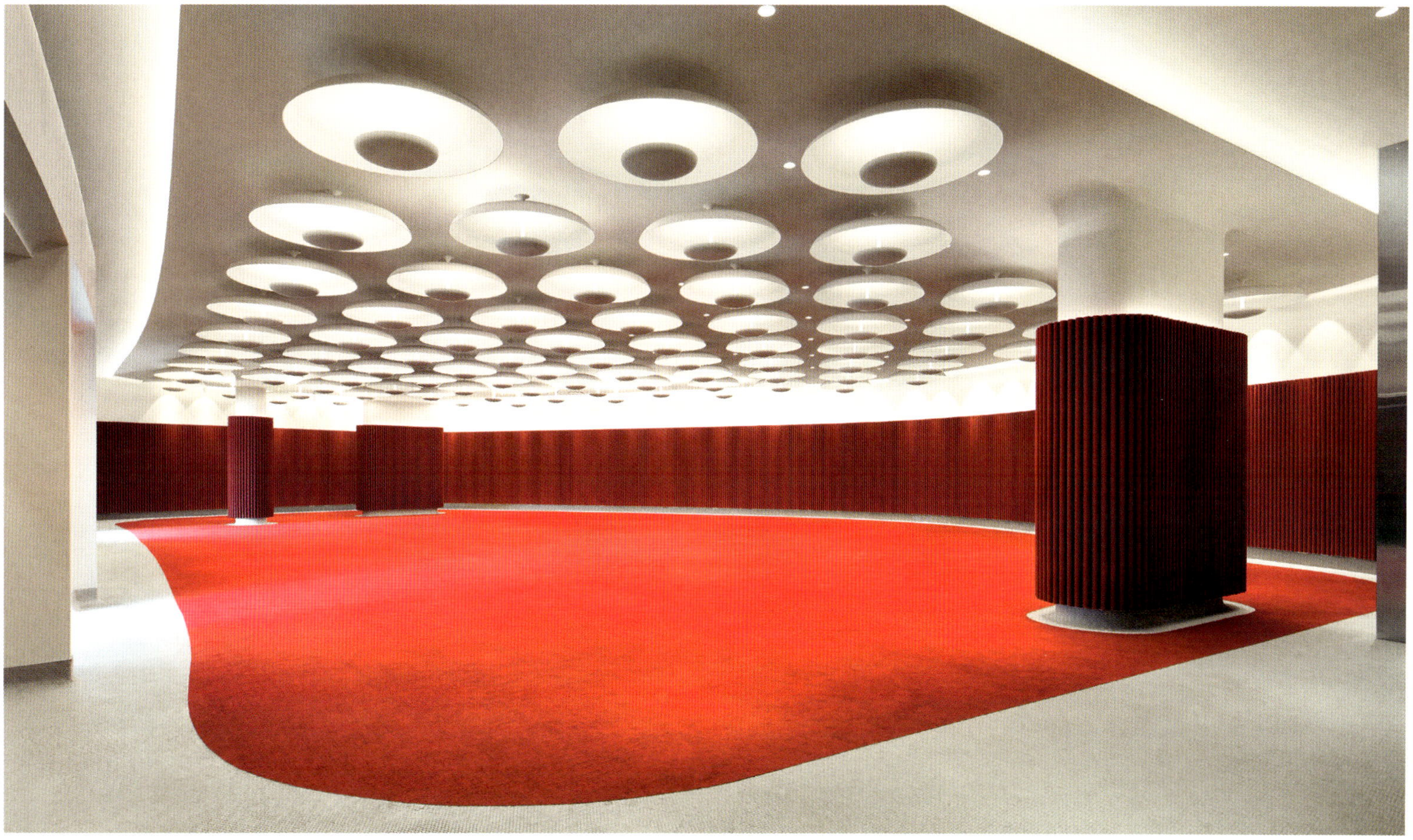

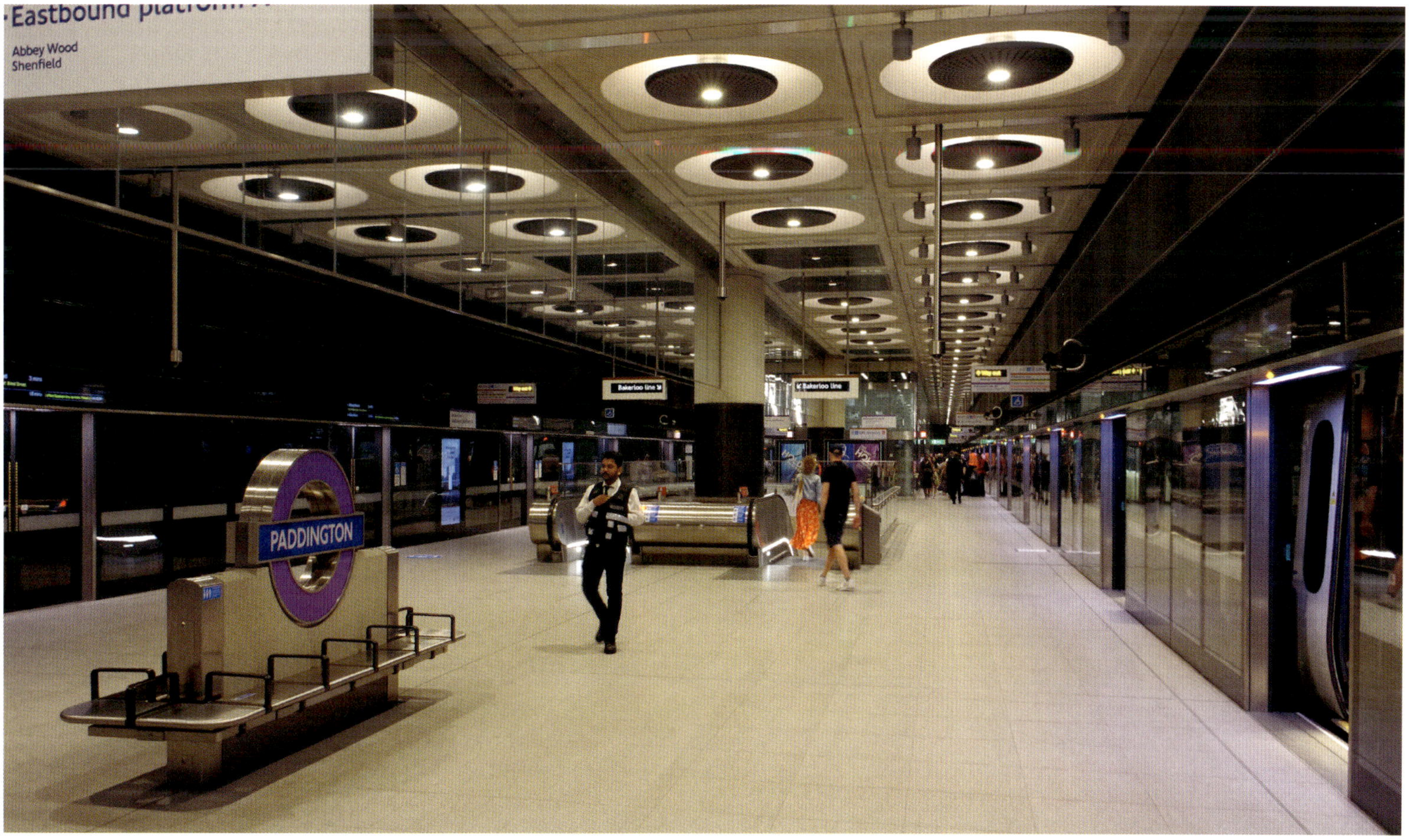
Eastbound
Abbey Wood
Shenfield
PADDINGTON
Bakerloo line
Bakerloo line

NASA LEH Space Shuttle Pressure helmet (Launch-Entry), used by Charlie Bolden, Johnson Space Center, Houston, [NASA], U.S.A., 2017.
Courtesy of the artist Vincent Fournier

Hoï Chan Kwok Chromatic Sofa, circa 1970 (© Michael Brunn), from the Downtown+ Trônes exhibion, Paris 2023

Enduring appeal: Fascination with iconic space-race-era design is not dissipating. San Francisco design collective and interior designers Studio Ahead feature the B&B Italia Camaleonda (top right) in their Noe Valley project, while B&B Italia's 50th-anniversary edition UP 50 (bottom right) remains central to their global product range. The Plasticarium in Brussels (above) has now become the permanent collection of Design Museum Brussels.

Contemporary L.A.-based designer Giampiero Tagliaferri is fast becoming one of the world's most in-demand interior stylists and creatives. "There are three pillars of my aesthetic," he says. "One being Chic. The next being Brutalism. And the other is Space-Age California." His Silver Lake project in Los Angeles is a classic example of his work, featuring Space-Age design and art against clean Modernist architecture.

Verner Panton retrospective at Trapholt Museum in Denmark, 2022. Design by Verner Panton, www.verner-panton.com © Verner Panton

SpaceX, one of a new generation of private space companies, executing a twin landing of the inaugural Falcon Heavy Stage 1 boosters, 2018

Mars Habitat by Hassell Architects

Interior by Peng Zheng of China's C&C Design, featured in the Andrew Martin International Interior Design Review Volume 26

"Most importantly, we found ourselves."

William P. Barry, former chief historian, NASA

THANKS AND ACKNOWLEDGMENTS

Discussing cold-war space strategy with NASA veterans and design history with curators of the world's great cultural institutions has been nothing less than an incredible privilege. My first thanks go to Stephanie Rebel, Roman Korn, and the team at the brilliant teNeues for their emphatic belief in this project and for being such positive and constructive partners. Thanks also to executive editor Dr. Thomas Hauffe for his invaluable help and guidance. I have huge gratitude to my Effetto colleagues. And my greatest thanks go to the interviewees, photographers, designers, galleries, brands, PRs, creatives, and individuals who have been so generous with their time and their work. Special thanks go to Dr. Teasel Muir-Harmony, curator of the Apollo Collection at the Smithsonian National Air and Space Museum in Washington D.C.; Dr Roger D. Launius, former chief historian of NASA; Johanna Agerman Ross, chief curator at the Design Museum in London; Cristina Bargna at Design Museum Brussels; Carin Panton von Halem for so generously opening the Verner Panton archives; Eero Aarnio, designer of the legendary Ball Chair, contributing to the project despite being in his late 90s; Benjamin and Alice Paulin for their time in Miami and their generosity with the Pierre Paulin archives; Vincent Fournier for his huge visual contribution; Stine Liv Buur from Vitra; William P. Barry, former NASA chief historian; Ligne Roset, B&B Italia; Arne Jacobsen family; Jason Wray; Morentz, Mass Modern, Modest, Stilnovo; Kooloo; City Furniture; Donald Albrecht, Dominic Lutyens for his advice, the Society of Authors for their help, and so many more.

I also want to thank John Kellett for his encouragement and positivity, Desmond Muckian for his visual advice, and Paul Kellett and Jat Sahota for their support.

Most of all, my heartfelt thanks to my family: my father for igniting my lifelong fascination with space, my mother for her absolute encouragement and belief, my sister for being the most generous of sounding boards, Robert and Sofia, and most of all, my wife Stefania and my daughter Beatrice for sharing me with this project for a year of evenings and weekends—this is for you.

ABOUT THE AUTHOR

Peter Martin is editor-in-chief of an international design, art and architecture publication and editorial director of a global marketplace for vintage and contemporary design and art. Before his career in journalism, he was a successful record producer and television advertising creative. He has edited and produced several books on design, interiors, art and architecture, and Space Age Design is his first authored book. He lives in London, UK.

PHOTO CREDITS

Airborne Archives: 108; Alamy: 109 (bottom), 236 (bottom); Alamy/Mauritius: 88; Artifort: 114, 115, 124; Artifort/Paulin family: 2, 46, 50, 51, 63; B&B Italia: 156, 176, 179, 182, 245 (bottom); B&B Italia/Klaus Zaugg: 157; Bayer: 178, 191; © Michael Brunn / Downtown+: 242, 243; Matt Buck/Flickr: 239 (bottom); C&C Design – Peng Zheng, as featured in the Andrew Martin International Interior Design Review Volume 26: 253; Chemosphere #2 by Squid Ink/ Creative Commons via Flickr: 26; Dr Peter James Chisholm: 25; City Furniture: 79, 127, 195; Cividino: Stephan Julliard/Gallery Clément Cividino/Famille Xasteros: 202, 203; Courtesy Davis Brody Bond, a Page company: 187, 188; De Sede: 219, 220; Design Museum Brussels: 151, 154, 192, 205; Design Museum Brussels/ Gufram: 120; Design Museum Brussels: Plasticarium: 244; Design Museum Brussels/Zanotta SpA Italy: 121; Eero Aarnio Archives: 94, 97, 129, 134; © Fine Art Images/Heritage Images/Alamy/Mauritius: 16, 17; Courtesy Vincent Fournier: 4, 34, 35, 37-39, 213, 230, 231, 240, 241; Fritz Hansen: 42; © Michael Furman: 64-65 (bottom), 162; Photo Sam Frost courtesy Giampiero Tagliaferri: 246, 247; GM Archive: 66,67; © The Guy Bourdin Estate 2024, Courtesy of Louise Alexander Gallery: 85; Peter Harholdt: 64-65 (top); Hassell: 252; Courtesy of Herman Miller Archive: 40; Courtesy of Knoll, Inc.: 54; Courtesy of Knoll Archives: 56; Kooloo Modern: 36, 126, 225; Joe Kramm: 153; Library of Congress/Balthazar Korab: 28, 100; Carol M. Highsmith Archive, Library of Congress, Prints and Photographs Division: 55; Ligne Roset: 222, 223, 228; Ligne Roset Archive: 136, 137; Los Angeles World Airports: 8, 9, 27; Peter Martin: 44; Mass Modern Design: 62, 158, 161, 173; Modest Furniture: 58, 60, 105, 109 (top), 163, 168, 197; Morentz: 43, 80, 190, 193; NASA: 6, 18-20, 22-24, 41, 52, 57, 59, 63, 68, 77, 78, 81, 82, 84, 86, 87, 89, 96, 101, 104, 110, 112, 117, 118, 122, 123, 125, 128, 132, 135, 144-148, 148, 150, 152, 155, 164-167, 169-171, 177, 183, 189, 194, 196, 198, 200, 201, 204, 206, 207, 214, 216, 218, 221, 224, 227, 232, 254; Oluce: 217; Paradisoterrestre: 180; Mattia Tonelli/Courtesy Paradisoterrestre: 106, 107, 181; Courtesy Paulin Paulin Paulin: 199; Courtesy Paulin Paulin Paulin/Château La Coste: 160; © Oppenheim/Courtesy Paulin Paulin Paulin: 159; Jean-Marie Périer/Photo12: 111; © Photo Pierre Cardin Evolution: 226 (top); PIG Design – Wenqiang li, as featured in the Andrew Martin International Interior Design Review Volume 26: 237; Harry Pot/Anefo: 45; Photograph by Rama, Wikimedia Commons, Cc-by-sa-2.0-fr: 95; Shutterstock: 53; Courtesy Danilo Silvestrin and thanks to Oliver Wolleh, lothar-walleh.com: 119; Stilnovo: 21; Studio AHEAD / Ekaterina Izmestiyeva: 245 (top); TATO: 29, 149; TWA Hotel: 32, 33, 239 (top); Unsplash/ Francesco Zivoli: 172; Unsplash: 236 (top); Unsplash/SpaceX: 250, 251; Various Associates: 238; © Verner Panton Design AG: 49, 83, 98, 99, 113, 116, 184-186, 248, 249; Verpan: Design by Verner Panton/© Verner Panton Design AG & Verpan A/S/Produced under license by Verpan A/S: 61, 69, 90-93, 174,175, 233; Vitra: Cone Chair by Verner Panton available from Vitra. Photography by Marc Eggimann © Vitra: 47, 48; Vitra: Panton Chair by Verner Panton available from Vitra: 102, 103; Jason Wray: 215; Zanotta SpA Italy: 130, 131; Gil Zetbase / Creative Commons: 226 (bottom)

Photographs Cover (front) from top left to bottom right: 1 Modest Furniture, Antwerp, 2 VP Globe pendant designed by Verner Panton, photo: Joe Kramm, 3 Verner Panton landscaped interior for the Visiona II exhibition in 1968. Design by Verner Panton, www.verner-panton.com
© Verner Panton, 4 NASA, 5 B&B Italia, 6 Design by Verner Panton / © Verner Panton Design AG / Produced under license by Verpan A/S, 7 TWA Hotel, 8 Modest Furniture, Antwerp. (back): Los Angeles World Airports. All rights reserved.

IMPRESSUM

1st printing

Concept and text by Peter Martin
Picture Editing by Peter Martin

Project Management and Copyediting by Thomas Hauffe
Design and Color Separation by Raw Color: Christoph Brach, Daniera ter Haar, Tijs Van Nieuwenhuysen, Jannie Guo (www.rawcolor.nl)
Proofreading by writehouse, Katrin Höller

Editorial Coordination by Stephanie Rebel, teNeues Verlag
Production by Sandra Jansen-Dorn, teNeues Verlag

ISBN: 978-3-96171-603-6

Library of Congress Cataloging-in-Publication data is available from the publisher.
Printed in the Czech Republik by PBtisk a.s.

Bibliographic information published by the Deutsche Nationalbibliothek: The Deutsche Nationalbibliothek lists this publication in the Deutsche Nationalbibliografie; detailed bibliographic data are available on the Internet at dnb.dnb.de.

Published by teNeues Publishing Group

teNeues Verlag GmbH
Ohmstraße 8a
86199 Augsburg, Germany

Düsseldorf Office
Waldenburger Straße 13
41564 Kaarst, Germany
e-mail: books@teneues.com

Augsburg/München Office
Ohmstraße 8a
86199 Augsburg, Germany
e-mail: books@teneues.com

Press Department
presse@teneues.com

teNeues Publishing Company
350 Seventh Avenue, Suite 1702
New York, NY 10001, USA
Phone: +1-212-627-9090
Fax: +1-212-627-9511

www.teneues.com

https://instagram.com/teneuespublishing

teNeues Publishing Group
Augsburg / München
Berlin
Düsseldorf
London
New York